Kurt Tucholsky

Germany? Germany!
Satirical Writings: The Kurt Tucholsky Reader

Germany? Germany!

Satirical Writings:
The Kurt Tucholsky Reader

Kurt Tucholsky

Translated by Harry Zohn

New York and Berlin, 2017

Berlinica

Germany? Germany!
Satirical Writings: The Kurt Tucholsky Reader
By Kurt Tucholsky
Translator: Harry Zohn
Editor: Eva C. Schweitzer

© 2017 by Berlinica Publishing LLC
255 West 43rd St., Suite 1012, New York, NY, 10036; USA

ISBN 978-1-935902-38-6
ISBN ebook
978-1-935902-39-3, 978-1-935902-48-5
LCCN 2016954769
ISBN Germany 978-3-96026-025-7

Cover photo from the famed Konnopke Currywurst locale
on Schönhauser Allee in Berlin's Prenzlauer Berg
Artist: Mural Art Berlin by Graco-Urban.de

Photos
p. 14: Steven Zohn
pp. 26, 64, 84: Public Domain
p. 122: Eva C. Schweitzer

www.berlinica.com

"Man is a creature that knocks, makes bad music, and lets his dog bark. Sometimes he leaves you in peace, but then he is dead. Besides men there are Saxons and Americans, but we won't take them up until next year when we have Zoology."

—*Kurt Tucholsky*

Contents

He's One of Us. Only More So

By Ralph Blumenthal

Is this America's Weimar? Ridiculous, you say. Have we sapped our youth in a ruinous war? Are bank savings vanishing? Are we looking for scapegoats like... foreigners? See, I told you. So please, dear sir and madam, ignore the hateful speeches, government paralysis, and seething electorate that's making for an ominous mood in a volatile political season, and by all means do not pick up this little time capsule from Kurt Tucholsky. It might upset you.

A brave and sly chronicler of Germany between the wars, Tucholsky (alias Peter Panter, Theobald Tiger, Ignaz Wrobel and Kaspar Hauser), was more than an astute eyewitness to history, and a very dark history at that. He was a puckish critic of the universal human comedy. His dispatches reach out meaningfully beyond his tragic era and across the generations to us. Eight decades after his suicide in Swedish exile in 1935 at age 45, he has much wisdom to share. We nod and smile, or grimace, and say, "yes, that's how it is, still."

In fact, Tucholsky gives us just such a shout-out in this volume, a prescient piece from 1926 called "To Posterity, Greetings." He fancies addressing the reader in the far distant future—1986. Sure, the fashions and expressions and gadgets will be different. But how well he knows us. He knows we haven't figured out the United Nations (he still calls it the League of Nations) or the "United States of Europe" (how true that is!). "Problems, you see aren't solved—just shelved—by mankind." And he ends with a chilling truth: "You aren't any better than we were, or those before us. Not in the least, not in the very least..."

Tucholsky was a quick-change artist. He committed journalism, travel-writing, satire, essays, criticism, poetry and play-writing—there's a fragment here from a farce about Columbus that he co-wrote with colleague Walter Hasenclever. In 1912, at 22, he also penned a sweet romance about a young Berlin couple, Claire and Wolfie, on a weekend tryst to the country. The real-life girlfriend and later wife, Else Weil whom he evokes so tenderly in "Rheinsberg, A Storybook for Lovers," would be put aboard a transport to Auschwitz and vanish in the Holocaust.

Tucholsky exemplifies what it is to be human. He doesn't exalt himself, "a little fat fellow" who has to get up on a footstool to kiss his too-tall girlfriend. (Yes, he had girlfriends, even when he was married—who said he was perfect?) You could say he fits the description of what the Israeli founder Chaim Weizmann (or someone else) may once have said about his tribe: Jews are like other people, only more so. Kurt Tucholsky is like us, only more so.

I'm no expert on Tucholsky. I came to him late in life and don't claim to know more than what I've picked up as an admiring reader and student of German history. (That's what we journalists do—gravely present the public with facts we ourselves learned only five minutes before). But you, like me, will quickly recognize a master in this towering little fellow who fearlessly skewered the evil of his time, along with the foibles of his ridiculous fellow humans.

Here he is on immigrants: "To most people a foreigner represents his state." So to a German hausfrau, a Chinese stranger she meets on the stairs becomes the embodiment of all China—opium dens, pirate braids, even geishas (OK, they're Japanese, but never mind). The same foreigner might be a "useless, pushed-around" nobody at home; but abroad "Everybody still behaves as if a powerful constituent of a completely unified tribe were coming to us…"

On borders: "And the thing they call Europe has become a multicolored patchwork, and a man is a foreigner if he so much as sticks his nose out of his village!" Tucholsky wrote that in 1920, nearly a century before hastily erected fences are penning up the waves of Syrian, Iraqi and Afghan migrants.

In Paris (where Tucholsky moved in 1924) he meets a bus driver who kindly gives him directions. Another time and "he would have lunged ahead and stuck his bayonet into my stomach." And so he wonders, "Will it start up again tomorrow? Will it?"

It will.

Tucholsky can also be quite funny. Have you heard the one about the husband and wife who try to tell him a joke? (Well they call him Herr Panter but, trust me, it's Tucholsky.) Anyway, there's this old peasant farmer married to a beautiful young thing. They're in bed when a stranger knocks at the door and — oh, wait they're not in bed yet but there's a storm and now someone's knocking — no, it's a phone call, that's what it is, and the husband goes out, he goes out to feed the goat, and the stranger—hold on, he's hungry and there's a little cheese left. Anyway, the stranger gets into bed with the young wife—this is when the husband is still outside and she— the young wife—pokes him—the stranger—and says, Well? No? She doesn't say "Well?" (Tucholsky—excuse me, Panter—never does find out what the young wife says to the stranger.)

He has advice for the German traveler: "You should by all means involve the ridiculous natives in an immediate discussion of politics, religion and the war. Don't hold back your opinion: speak out freely! Give it to them! Speak loudly so they can hear you; a lot of foreigners are hard of hearing, anyway."

Who else would create a talking embryo? "I'm supposed to slumber for nine months, to take it easy—they wish me well... the church, the state, the physicians, the judges." Heaven help anyone who does this little fetus harm. "But once these nine months are past, I am on my own." No food, no milk, no medical care. "The church consoles me but does not fill my stomach." What's left? A life of crime.

Germans love playing with their toy soldier sets, the tiny tin figures on horseback, the little haystacks and fences and wells. "Here's what's missing," Tucholsky writes, "one half-decayed corpse: same, without head; two French wounded, with intestines hanging out..."

Don't say I didn't warn you. Tucholsky gives it to you with the bark on. He's one of us, only more so.

Ralph Blumenthal is a former correspondent of The New York Times, *the author of four non-fiction books, and a Distinguished Lecturer at Baruch College of the City University of New York.*

Harry Zohn, the Vienna-born translator, who brought Kurt Tucholsky to America.

A Heckling Voice in the Gallery and the Conscience of Germany

By Harry Zohn

Holden Caulfield, the protagonist of J.D. Salinger's novel *The Catcher in the Rye*, once said that whenever he liked an author very much, he felt like calling him up on the telephone. I have felt that way about Kurt Tucholsky for decades. So, like Tucholsky's creation Herr Wendriner, I shall say: "Operator! Give me…"

Possibly the most striking thing about the posthumous fame of the German Jewish journalist, satirist, and social critic is that those who know his work are inclined to class him in the first rank of satirists (according to the Berlin-born American critic Ludwig Lewisohn, "he belongs with Aristophanes, with Swift, with Heine, with Lucian among the few quite supreme masters of both mordant and laughing satire and irony"), but that the difficulties of translation and the vagaries of the literary and theatrical marketplace have largely excluded Tucholsky from present day interest in the culture of the Weimar Republic. For all too many readers in English-speaking countries that culture is defined only by such works as *The Threepenny Opera* by Bertolt Brecht and Kurt Weill, and Marlene Dietrich's film *The Blue Angel*. From 1918 to 1933, the lifespan of the ill-starred republic, Tucholsky was the heckling voice in the gallery, and more than that: the conscience of Germany. A man of uncompromising principles and consistent honesty, of many tensions and conflicting traits—by turns playful and serious, timid and aggressive, coarse and lyrical, self critical and skeptical, melancholy and buoyant—Tucholsky possessed a remarkable clairvoyance as to the shape of things to come. His clear recognition of the suicidal madness of his epoch proved to be his undoing, for Tucholsky took his own life only a few years after his brilliant career had been cut off by the Nazis' accession to power. This tragic act may have been due to his realization that the Nazi dictatorship would be overcome only by that other monster against which he had fought so passionately throughout his creative life: war. That very sensitive man may not have wished to stay around long enough to be confronted by a choice between these two evils.

Kurt Tucholsky had Berliners in mind in many of his writings, but his work transcends the limits of his own period and language by virtue of its truth to human nature. Tucholsky's output is sketchy, essentially anthological, consisting mainly of lively short pieces, essays, critiques, reportages, monologues, poems, aphorisms, and glosses that often employ the peppery idiom of the common man, which is the hallmark of much great satire.

Kurt Tucholsky (pronounced too-KHOL-skee) was born in Berlin on January 9, 1890, as the son of a prosperous Jewish businessman. At the age of nine he entered the French Gymnasium there, a Huguenot-founded institution that instilled in him some of the Gallic spirit and an abiding love of France; his linguistic prowess, lucid style, and clear reasoning derive from this education. In 1908, Tucholsky enrolled at the University of Berlin; he also studied in Geneva and in 1915 earned a doctorate of laws from the University of Jena. Shortly thereafter he was conscripted into the German army; his three and a half years of service on the Eastern front made him an ardent pacifist. Twice he was married for short periods, the second time to Mary Gerold, whom he had met while on military duty. (His second marriage ended in 1928, but he was wise enough to appoint Frau Mary as the executor of his estate.) During most of his later years, from 1924 to his suicide on 21 December 1935, Tucholsky lived outside Germany, mainly in France, Switzerland, and Sweden. It may be characteristic of Tucholsky the man and the satirist that the two poles of his literary creativity—*Rheinsberg, ein Bilderbuch für Verliebte* (Rheinsberg, a Picture Book for Lovers, 1912, a fanciful and witty account of a weekend trip of two urban lovers to a small town), and *Schloss Gripsholm* (Gripsholm Castle, 1931)—are not satirical works but charming, tender, gently ironic love idylls that blend the melancholy charm of the late nineteenth century with the brash wit prevalent among Berlin society in the early years of this century and between the wars. Tucholsky the inveterate traveller and gifted reporter is seen to good advantage in *Ein Pyrenäenbuch* (A Book About the Pyrenees, 1927), which contains an account of the Catholic shrine of Lourdes and the miracle of Bernadette's grotto that antedates Franz Werfel's celebrated novel by more than a decade.

In 1913 Tucholsky became associated with *Die Schaubühne* (The Stage), later called *Die Weltbühne* (The World Stage). This publication began as a theatrical and literary magazine but soon became one of the most aggressive satirical-political periodicals of the time. Although Tucholsky contributed to a variety of other publications, the *Weltbühne* remained the principal vehicle for his poems, glosses, anecdotes, aphorisms, critiques, philosophical essays, and critical attacks upon the foibles of his society and the resurgent German nationalism and militarism. When the editor of the *Weltbühne*, his friend and mentor Siegfried Jacobsohn, died unexpectedly in 1926, "Tucho" briefly took over the editorship of this publication, but the indefatigable cosmopolitan soon found the editor's chair too confining and turned his duties over to Carl von Ossietzky, another staunch anti-militarist who was to receive the Nobel Peace Prize in 1935 while languishing in a Nazi concentration camp.

Kurt Tucholsky was a "man with five heads," for his writings appeared under five names. In addition to his own name he used the pseudonyms Peter Panter, Theobald Tiger, Ignaz Wrobel, and Kaspar Hauser. These were not chosen or employed capriciously or motivated by cowardice; rather, they were intended to be symbolic of the satirist's many-faceted personality and the diversity of his thought. Panter and Tiger were not meant to suggest the ferocity of wild animals; one of Tucholsky's law teachers had coined such alliterative animal names as equivalents of our John Doe. *Mit 5 PS*, the title of Tucholsky's 1928 collection that could mean either "With Five Horsepower" or "Under Five Pseudonyms," alludes to what the author called his "cheerful schizophrenia." He found it useful to be present five times, as it were, "for who in Germany believes that a political writer is capable of humor or that a satirist can be serious? Who would credit a playful man with knowledge of the penal code, or who would believe that a describer of cities can write light verse? Humor discredits a man." Tucholsky's account of the "funeral" of

"Kaspar Theobald Peter Kurt lgnaz Wrobel" ends with a collective epitaph that could also stand for Kurt Tucholsky, the man and the writer: "Here lie a heart of gold and a jaw of iron. Good night…"

It is a tribute to Tucholsky's stature that a comparison with Heinrich Heine, the foremost satirist of nineteenth-century German literature, readily suggests itself. Tucholsky certainly considered himself a kindred spirit of the poet, and there are several parallels in their writings and personal lives. Both Heine and Tucholsky were primarily journalists, and both had been law students before they became writers. Both were employees of a bank for some time; both loved France, where they spent part of their lives. Both writers were born Jews and left the Jewish fold in their twenties, without practicing the Christian religion or even believing in it. Like Heine, Tucholsky died in exile; when he thought of Germany by night, sleep would not come to him, we have reason to assume—a situation to which Heine gave such poignant lyrical expression in his poem "Night Thoughts." In both Heine and Tucholsky qualities of tenderness and delicacy are blended with a razor-sharp aggressiveness. In his analytical attitude, his militant intellectuality and wit, and his non-observance of tradition, Tucholsky displayed an affinity with the "Young Germany" movement to which Heine was close in the 1830s.

Like Heine, Tucholsky was a true humorist; behind his jibes and quips there lies a deep seriousness. One of Tucholsky's aphorisms is timely when militarists are routinely honored but the powers that be were reluctant to name the University of Düsseldorf after that city's greatest son: "In Germany, the number of war memorials is to the number of Heine memorials as force is to the spirit."

Tucholsky also felt an affinity with Lucian (Lukianos), the most brilliant and witty satirist of Greek letters under the Roman Empire. The thrusts of his typewriter were sharp and well aimed, but he himself imposed certain restrictions on the range of his targets. In 1929 he wrote: "Satire has a limit at the top; Buddha is above it. It also has a limit at the bottom: the Fascist forces in Germany. It doesn't pay—one can't shoot that low." (This foreshadows the resignation of Karl Kraus, Tucholsky's Viennese Counterpart, and his frequently misinterpreted statement of a few years later, "Mir fällt zu Hitler nichts ein"—I can't think of anything to say about Hitler—expressing the incommensurability of brutishness with the human spirit.) And thus Tucholsky, an implacable foe of National Socialism and everything it stood for, was less vocal in his attacks on the Hitler movement than he might have been, like so many others underestimating the full fury to come. He was less restrained in his criticism of the German Social Democrats for their vacillations, compromises, and perceived betrayal of the 1918 revolution. This endeared him to the Communists, but Tucholsky never joined their party or any other, except for a brief affiliation with a Socialist splinter group in the early 1920s—for the Tucholskys (and Krauses) of the world are in a class by themselves, and no viable political organization can offer a program wholly in keeping with their views. He opposed organized religion, but he rarely referred to God in an irreverent manner—especially in his later writings—and evidently did not consider it reactionary to invoke his assistance.

Tucholsky never crossed the Atlantic Ocean (his brother Fritz emigrated to the United States and perished in an automobile accident a few years after Kurt's demise; his sister Ellen Milo lived to a ripe old age in New York), and so his image of America as a cold and mercenary country was necessarily incomplete and distorted; the ending of the last scene of the Hasenclever-Tucholsky play *Christopher Columbus* (p. 110) is probably an exercise in irony. Still, Tucholsky's indictment of the American penal system is as valid as if it had been composed by a native of Massachusetts. Some sixty years after "To Posterity, Greetings" was written, who can deny that in the post-1985 world vested interests override human considerations as ruthlessly as they did in Tucholsky's time? Yet even the satirist could not have foreseen how perilously close to fulfillment his tongue-in-cheek prediction was to come (see his spoof on "Germany's Lamplighters," p. 37) that, some day, German light would glow in Strasbourg, Danzig, Vienna, Budapest, and New York. And in other respects history has even gone one better (or worse): "Wouldn't we today split our sides laughing," he asks in "The Border" (p. 66), "at someone who'd urge us to break down the barriers between Berlin and Magdeburg?" Today such a barrier does exist; it is known as the Berlin Wall, and hardly anybody finds its existence a laughing matter.

Among Tucholsky's best remembered (and most controversial) works is a series of sixteen monologues devoted to the thoughts and doings of Herr Wendriner, one of his most felicitous and most memorable characterizations. Wendriner is the personification of a Berlin businessman of Jewish origin, a lightweight in mind and morals who speaks in clipped Prussian accents and swallows his syllables as well as his thoughts in a perpetuum mobile of the tongue. These "psycho-monologues" are a running commentary on the Weimar Republic and convey to us the world of the Babbits of Tucholsky's time. The figure of Wendriner is a sort of safety valve for the Hassliebe (love-hate) that Tucholsky felt for Germany, Berlin, and his fellow Jews, whom he wanted to jar out of their complacency. "I don't love Berlin," he wrote shortly before his death; "God tasted her Wendriners and immediately spat them out again." The monologue "Herr Wendriner Under the Dictatorship" (p. 56), written on the eve of Hitler's accession to power, finally cuts this figure down to size, exposing the business-as-usual attitude of the spiritually empty assimilated Jew; in his unctuous, propitiatory servility he is quite ready to make his peace with the Nazis if they will only let him carry on.

Tucholsky was one of the first prominent German Jewish intellectuals to take his own life, and the possible relationship between his Jewishness and his final tragedy has been noted. "In Kurt Tucholsky's love of Germany," wrote Ludwig Lewisohn, "there was fatalism and tragic guilt, guilt toward himself, guilt toward the Jewish people." More recently the Jewish scholars Walter Laqueur (a native of Breslau) and Gershom Scholem (like Lewisohn and Tucholsky Berlin-born) have attempted to cast Tucholsky in the role of a Jewish anti-Semite.

Tucholsky never denied his Jewish origin, but in a letter dated 4 May 1929 he wrote: "The Jewish question has never really agitated me. From my writings you can see that I very seldom touch upon this area, my knowledge of which is not very great. I don't know whether the Zionists are on the right track or not, so I keep silent. People who want to hurt the Jew in me are usually wide of the mark." Early on Tucholsky referred to himself as "a Jew without religion," and near the end of his life he made this admission: "In 1911, I 'cancelled my membership' in Jewry, but I know that this can't be done." In his poignant farewell letter of December 15, 1935, to the writer Arnold Zweig, who had written to the satirist from his refuge in Palestine in an effort to draw him out of his shell, Tucholsky severely criticizes German Jews for passively accepting the idea of a ghetto and feck-lessly clinging to false hopes. "A deeply wounded soul was displayed," commented Zweig, "wounded not as a leftist, an intellectual, or a Cassandra-like prophet, but as a Jew."

Tucholsky's light verse, much of it in the Berlin dialect, is rarely the wonderful nonsense of Dorothy Parker, Ogden Nash, Edward Lear, Christopher Morley, or Arthur Guiterman. Much of it may be regarded as satires in lyric form—witty and irreverent, some-times quite angry and radical in tone. Tucholsky thought of these poems, some of which were recited or sung at workers' meetings, as *Gebrauchslyrik*, poetry for use, and they range from versified po-lemics to ironic-frivolous love poems. As a writer of Bänkellieder and political chansons and couplets (cabaret songs), Tucholsky may be compared with Bertolt Brecht, Frank Wedekind, Erich Kästner, Klabund, Joachim Ringelnatz, Walter Mehring, Robert Gilbert, and Mascha Kaleko. Many of Tucho's cabaret-type poems were writ-ten for revues like *Bitte Zahlen* (Check, Please), *Wir stehn verkehrt* (We're Facing the Wrong Way), and *Total Manoli* (Plumb Crazy).

The music for these shows was written by Rudolf Nelson. Other prominent composers who supplied musical settings in Tucholsky's lifetime included Hans May, Werner Richard Heymann, Friedrich Holländer, and Mischa Spoliansky; among the noted composers inspired by his work after World War II were Hanns Eisler, Olaf Bienert, and Henry Krtschil (the last-named in East Germany). Tucholsky himself wrote the music for some of his lyrics; "Worte und Musik von Theobald Tiger" was once a familiar notation on the program of fabled cabarets like *Schall und Rauch* (Sound and Smoke). Many of Tucholsky's poems and chansons were written for well-known performers, who frequently recited or sang them on the stage. These included Rosa Valetti, Ernst Busch, Kate Kühl, Gussy Holl, Paul Graetz, Trude Hesterberg, Blandine Ebinger, Ernestine Coster, Nina Consta, Annemarie Hase, Käthe Erlholz, Mady Chris-tians, Grethe Weiser, and Claire Waldoff. Some of these artists survived the Nazi inferno and revived this material in post war theatres, concert halls, and cabarets. In this endeavour they were joined on the stage and in the recording studio by such younger actors, actresses, and singers as Eva Busch, Martin Held, Hildegard Knef, Erich Schellow, Gerd Vespermann, Gisela May, Norbert Gescher, Johanna von Koczian, Ralf Linnemann, Hannes Messemer, Helen Vita, and Wolfgang Reichmann.

Possibly Tucholsky's most famous work is his mordant picture book *Deutschland, Deutschland Über Alles*, produced in 1929 in collaboration with the commercial artist and master of photomontage John Heartfield (originally Helmut Herzfeld) as well as many photographers. This book of prose, poetry, and pictures graphically catches Germany (and holds her in suspended animation, as it were) at a critical moment in history, a few years before the philistinism, brutality, perversion, cupidity, and stupidity rampant in public life were to produce the tragedy of Nazism. The book presents what Marcel Belvianes has called "a sociology of the photograph"; it contains not only photos of the "muck-raking" variety, but also ingenious pictorial devices that have since been widely imitated. Most of the accustomed targets of Tucholsky's satire are there: the strutting, justice-defying, arbitrary, capricious exploiters of all sorts, the officer caste and the judges, the great moloch State that intimidates and subdues the individual, but also such less momentous aspects of German life as the grinding ugliness of the environment, and traffic regulations that are not utilitarian but designed to bring into play the German mania for asserting authority and obeying it.

Inevitably, the book was widely discussed and gained Tucholsky many new enemies. Had he not dragged into the mud the refrain of the German national anthem (which he called "that fatuous verse of a big-mouthed poem"), and was he not stunting the growth of that fragile flower, the Weimar Republic, with his satiric sniping? It should be noted, however, that Tucholsky closed his pandaemonium Germanicum with an essay entitled "Heimat" in which he drew a distinction between patriotism and love of one's fatherland. "We have a right to hate Germany." he wrote, "because we love it." Tucholsky viewed himself as a representative of "the quiet love of our homeland—without flags, hurdy-gurdies, sentimentality, and a drawn sword." For the rest, he had answered his critics as early as 1919, when he had responded to his own question "What may satire do?" by writing: "Anything. Satire must exaggerate, and it is in its innermost nature to be unjust. It inflates truth to make it more distinct, and it cannot help but operate in accordance with the biblical saying that the just suffer along with the unjust."

By the time that book appeared, its author had chosen Sweden as his permanent domicile. A letter of May 5, 1931, contains these revealing remarks: "What sometimes worries me so is the effectiveness of my work. Does it have any? (I don't mean success; that leaves me cold)... I write and work—and what practical effect does it have on the way the country is run? Do I get a single one of those foul, perverted, tormented and tormenting female wardens fired? Do the sadists leave? Are the bureaucrats dismissed? This is what depresses me at times." Several recently published volumes of Tucholsky's letters and diaries make for excruciating reading, for they give stark evidence of the satirist's mounting depression and despair. His feeling of frustration and insecurity was exacerbated by severe sinus trouble that was not alleviated by operations. A few weeks before his forty-sixth birthday, Tucholsky, a lapsed German Jew and a lapsed writer in exile, a man who had despaired of a society without democratic traditions, sought "the truest of all democracies, the democracy of death" by taking poison. Tucholsky is buried in Mariefred cemetery, near the castle, which he immortalized in literature.

Kurt Tucholsky's posthumous fame is at once a gratifying and a disturbing phenomenon—gratifying because in recent decades this excellent writer has had a far greater readership than he enjoyed in his lifetime, disturbing because more than a half-century after he stopped writing his work is deemed to be of undiminished timeliness and relevance—in fact, doubly necessary in an age that has produced no great satirist. In both West and East Germany Tucholsky is published in a manner befitting a modern classic; millions of copies of his books have been sold, numerous dissertations and other studies have been written about him, and he is a living presence on the stage, in cinemas, in the concert hall, in the press, in the cabaret, and in the homes and hearts of countless readers.

Tucholsky is noted for his Juvenalian (hard-hitting) as well as his

Horatian satire (the more gentle kind), and the present collection is intended to present examples of both, aiming at that "thoughtful laughter" which George Meredith considered to be the true index of the comic spirit. May this Reader, which is greatly indebted to the late Mary Tucholsky and to the Rowohlt Verlag, the satirist's publisher then and now, promote the English-speaking world's appreciation of a rare creative spirit.

Harry Zohn (1923-2001) emigrated as a Viennese Jew to England in 1939 and to Boston, Massachusetts in 1940. He earned his Ph.D. at Harvard and taught at Brandeis University from 1951 to 1996. A prolific author, editor, and translator, his work focused on Austrian- and German-Jewish literature of the late nineteenth and early twentieth centuries. This introduction was written, under a different title, for the 1989 edition.

Part I
Germany? Germany!

Kurt Tucholsky was born in Berlin in 1890 and died in Mariefred, Sweden, in 1935. The picture is from 1928.

To Posterity, Greetings

Gruß nach Vorne, 1926

D ear Reader of the Year 1985:
Through some chance you are rummaging in the library; you come across this volume, pause, and read. Greetings.

I am very self-conscious. You are wearing a suit of a fashion that contrasts greatly with the one I used to wear, and you carry your cranium quite differently too. I make three starts—each time with a different subject; after all, we've got to establish contact... Each time I have to give it up again; we don't understand each other at all. It must be that I am too small; my era reaches up to my neck, my head barely sticks out a little bit above the level of my time... There, I knew it—you're smiling me down.

Everything about me seems old-fashioned to you: my way of writing and my grammar and my attitude. Oh, don't slap my back; I don't like that. I'm trying in vain to tell you how things were with us and how we made out... Nothing... You smile, my voice sounds ineffectively from the past, and you know everything better. Shall I tell you what people in my chronological neck of the woods got excited about? Geneva? A Shaw premiere? Thomas Mann? Television? A steel island in the ocean as an aircraft base? You snort at everything and the dust flies yard-high; you can't recognize a thing because of all that dust.

Shall l flatter you? I can't. Of course you haven't solved the problem "League of Nations or United States of Europe?" Problems, you see, aren't solved—just shelved—by mankind. Naturally, you have in your daily life three hundred trivial gadgets more than we had, and, for the rest, you are just as stupid, just as smart, just as we were. What of us has remained? Don't burrow in your memory, among those things you learned in school. What has remained is what stayed by accident, what was so neutral that it made it across; of what is really great, about one half has remained—and no one gives a hoot about that, except, maybe, on Sunday morning, in a museum. It is just as if today I were supposed to speak with a man from the Thirty Years' War. "Oh? Are you all right? Must have been pretty draughty during the siege of Magdeburg...," and the other things one says.

I can't even carry on a high-level conversation with you over the heads of my contemporaries, with the theme: We two understand each other, for you are an intellectual, like me. Alas, my good friend—you are somebody's contemporary, too. Of course, when I say "Bismarck" and you have to think hard of who that was, I break out in a grin even today. You can't imagine how proud the people around me are of that man's immortality. Oh well, let's drop that. Besides, you'll want to go and have your lunch now.

So long, then. This paper has turned quite yellow, yellow like the teeth of our county judges—look, the page is crumbling between your fingers; well, it is rather old. Go with God, or whatever you call that thing now. We probably don't have too much to say to one another, we little people. We are lived out, our essence has passed away with us. The appearance was everything.

Oh yes. I want to shake your hand. For the sake of good manners. And now you're off.

But let me tell you one more thing: You aren't any better than we were, or those before us. Not in the least, not in the very least...

A Fable

Märchen, 1907

There was once an emperor who ruled over an immeasurably large, rich, and beautiful country. And like any other emperor, he also had a treasure room, which in addition to all the sparkling jewels contained a snuffbox. But it was a strange kind of snuffbox. What remarkable things were depicted on its lid! There was a landscape, small but full of life: a Thoma landscape with Böcklin clouds and Leistikow lakes. Reznicek-like ladies turned up their noses at Zille figures, and a peasant maid a là Meunier carried an armful of Orlik flowers—in short, the whole artistic avant-garde was on this snuffbox.

And what do you suppose the emperor did with it? He sneezed at it.

In order to show how this piece had to be restyled in order to reproduce the verbal humor, the original is given below—H.Z.

Es war einmal ein Kaiser, der über ein unermesslich grosses, reiches und schönes Land herrschte. Und er besass wie jeder andere Kaiser auch eine Schatzkammer, in der inmitten all der glänzenden und glitzernden Juwelen auch eine Flöte lag. Das war aber ein merkwürdiges Instrument. Wenn man nämlich durch eins der vier Löcher in die Flöte hineinsah—oh! was gab es da alles zu sehen! Da war eine Landschaft darin, klein, aber voll Leben: Eine Thoma'sche Landschaft mit Böcklin'schen Wolken und Leistikow'schen Seen. Reznicek'sche Dämchen rümpften die Nasen über Zille'sche Gestalten, und eine Bauerndirne Meuniers trug einen Arm voll Blumen Orliks—kurz, die ganze "moderne" Richtung war in der Flöte.

Und was machte der Kaiser damit? Er pfiff drauf.

Face of a German

Gesicht, 1924

To George Grosz, who taught us to see such faces.

A rather thick-set head; a none-to-high forehead; cold, small eyes; a nose that likes to lower itself into a drinking glass; a mouth used to snapping orders; a disagreeable toothbrush-like moustache: that's how this face looks. A well-cut black coat, a conservatively looped necktie with a sort of pearl in it, an always-clean collar: these also can be seen. The hair is cut short around the ears; the whole man is well scrubbed, cleans his fingernails in the morning, shaves or has the barber do it.

As a young man he pushed his way through the doors of lecture rooms, none too interested. His mama said to him: "Hubert, when will you be home today?" And he gave her a not very pleasant answer. He crammed. Passed exams. Was called upon in class— "Hubert So and So." And then he rose, a bit subservient, a bit worried, not very excited—cold, come to think of it. Entered government service, was promoted rapidly.

Long forenoons with difficult paper work, with empty breaks during which a snack was taken out of his briefcase; in it there also was an angry letter and one that promised a little off-duty enjoyment in the evening. For the rest: cold to his heart. Read a book once in a while that was not part of his work; tried Spengler once, crazy stuff; went to see Hardt's Tantris with the lady who wrote that letter. Very poetic.

Intermission: "It's possible that I'll be shifted to another department one of these days. Well, thank God..."

Company commander in the war. Hard as nails, cold. Cold toward the office boys who couldn't defend themselves, cold toward the young clerks ("Had to go through this myself once!"), cold toward the world, cold toward God. Married. Has two children. Loves them in his fashion. Likes to laugh sometimes, in the evening, at some fat joke; still knows three verses of that ballad about the innkeeper's wife, unfortunately has forgotten the rest. Firm-as-a-rock conviction of the justness of the state's structure, the legal system, the Church, and moral foundations in general. Hasn't given these things much thought. Doesn't look bad sitting there at the desk and briefly clearing his throat as he puts his many papers in order… After all, he is somebody. Feels in complete harmony with country, majority, and ethnic community. Not overly fond of the Prussian aristocracy, finds it disagreeable. But he is impeccably correct and polite, definitely a small bourgeois toward his superiors. To his underlings he is an aristocrat himself.

Plays the part. Advances his career. Will probably soon be some big shot—ambassador, head of a government department, secretary of state, or what-have-you.

Germany? Germany!

In One Sentence

Ein Satz, 1925

If, at a party, among a lot of nice, open, friendly clear-eyed people who chat easily, look honest, and exude no dignity whatever, you see a man who, with his chest thrown out, trumpets forth each word, letting two beady, cold eyes set in a low forehead flash forth imperiously, even with no serfs present, because he cares nothing about being important, but everything about being more important than anyone else, a man who wears a ribbon in his buttonhole and perhaps has a badly healed scar on his cheek, who squeezes on a monocle when he wants to read something that he won't understand anyway, a man who looks cowardly and brutal at the same time and whose entire bearing is redolent of a barely civilized slaughterhouse hand who is about to start a row on the dance floor, a man who is determined to bring the full force of his personality to bear on the most idiotic cause and who has so much prestige that nothing is left for humaneness, who, being a hollow shell himself, crawls into hiding behind his title, his decorations, his social standing which he rigidly emphasizes even when sitting down, a man who feels good only when he can be impressive with the riding whip among fellows who can't read or write but feed off him, and who takes care not to step into other social circles because there one would shrug him off with a smile, a man who isn't above taking money with well mani-cured, somewhat too fat fingers even from Jewish bankers if there's some profit in it, and who uses the wine waiter, this truckling tip-taker before the throne of his vanity, to reflect his power, a man who hides behind the state when he has pulled something off or wants to get a pension—if you see a man like that, you can bet your life that this man is a nationalist.

A Little Man Outside a Tavern

Kleiner Mann vor der Weinstube, 1922

One night at 12.30 p.m. I was outside a tavern on Potsdam Square. Things were really swinging—hey, hey! Inside, the people gagged by the shameful Treaty of Versailles were getting high as kites; those who came out exuded bad alcohol from their pores, and their eyes were lightly glazed, as though they had been listening to a lecture by Rudolf Steiner the theosophist. Now and then a tipsy couple came out of the place like two balls shot out of a cannon—she laughing constantly and he talking away both cheerfully and irately. Whereupon they disappeared Cytheraward... And inside the schnapps battle raged on.

Outside the window, in which there was a splendid array of a few empty bottles, stood a tiny, ragged man. He had no collar and was dressed from tip to toe in a crust of dirt that a very lenient observer might have called a suit. It probably had been a suit once. The man had gay little eyes, but he was completely sober. A small, friendly moustache was discreetly placed under his nose.

There he stood, listening to the joyous noise in the liquor-serving establishment. And each time there was a particularly loud roar from a man full of sweet wine, he shook his head cheerfully and his shoulders twitched. His whole little body shook with amusement. After all, he was quite sober, but he rejoiced that there still were people with enough money to get stinking drunk. He had no money to buy himself intoxication, so he got high on the tipsiness of others. So there still were such people—thank God! And the little man beamed.

I stood there for twenty minutes, watching him. At every din, every commotion, every battle cry, which the taxed liquid elicited from thirsty throats, he gave a start and had a good time. After twenty minutes he left—light of heart, deeply satisfied, and happy as a lark; he had had a marvelous time, and now he was going home in the best of spirits. A contented outsider was looking in on the good times of others—which made him a citizen right after Hergt's and Helfferich's hearts.*

---

* Oskar Hergt and Karl Helfferich were Prussian ministers of finance and leaders of the German National People's Party.—H.Z.

What If—?

Was wäre, wenn… ?, 1919

Posito, suppose… let us assume that we had won the war, by some crazy accident we had won it, the soldiers had come home (but had been detained in their barracks for months, as planned), and Kaiser Wilhelm II, after all that tumult, had departed his life—say, at the age of sixty-five—whereupon the Crown Prince had succeeded to the throne.

My God, the things that would have happened! Crown princes are always a clean slate, but this one would have been filled up in a hurry. The professors, who can prove anything because they have been trained to do so—well, the professors would have proved that Germany couldn't have had a more suitable, a more efficient, a better potentate than this young man. The exegetes would have come along and reasoned thus: from the young ruler's association with the best sportsmen of our time it follows that he intends to do everything for the physical training of the German youth, which is a great boon for Germany, for recruits are more important than men. And back and forth—what will you bet? In no time at all the man would have become extremely popular. His fast life as a student; his unexpressive face, that of a high society tennis player; his good figure; a few rumors about little love affairs emanating from Bann and Charleroi; all those sons of his (imagine what wonderful material for cabaret songs has been lost here!). In short: he would have been the man of the hour! The people would have cheered him and said to astonished foreigners: "You envy us our Emperor an awful lot, don't you? Oh well, there isn't another one like him!" And all monarchists would have beamed, because they had told us so…

Well, things happened a little differently. The unrestrained enthu-

siasm, which is always ready in certain men's bosoms, keeps wither-
ing away, because there is no Hohenzollern scion to extol—poor
bosoms! But there is another thing.

The same young man who would surely have been praised to the
skies if he had become Emperor now finds himself in a situation,
which displays the whole man—namely, misfortune. That would
have been a chance for a man to show what he really is, to observe a
manly silence, to stand up to fate and say: "I am going down—but
honorably!"

Instead of that, we are witnessing a spectacle too pitiful for words.
The go-getter who used to mount glorious attacks against newspapers he didn't care for (at Langemarck the majority of those who fell
were commoners) today hangs around the foreign correspondents
and begs for a favorable image: it wasn't he... he had told Dad...
Dad! How cute that sounds! Ludendorff was the one who...

Truth often comes late. But this one truth should not come too
late for us: the leader of a nation must not be the donation of a
ridiculous accident. But he must be chosen. Fortuna, the moody
goddess, almost put this man on our throne, adorned with all the
trappings of an obsolete profession. He now stands before us stark
naked: a skinny, pitiful little figure. What would have happened
if... ? Unthinkable.

Let us be glad that at least we have been saved from having had a
man on the German Emperor's throne who had no flaws of character because he had no character.

Germany's Lamplighters

Die Laternenanzünder, 1925

Many a reader may have wondered how the street lamps that illuminate our big cities night after night are activated. Well, comma, this question can be answered without too much difficulty. Surely the questioner has observed bands of two or three men with long poles who walk along the city streets every evening. They are lamplighters carrying out their difficult task. Who are these people, what are they doing so late on the dark streets, what are the requirements for their profession, and what is their training? To enlighten the reader on these points is the purpose of this article.

A lamplighter team is usually composed of three men: the chief lamplighter, his deputy, and the assistant lamplighter.

The chief lamplighter is the leader of the group. He bears the responsibility as well as a long pole and decides what lamps are to be lit. After "photoscoping"—that is the technical term—a particular street with light meter in hand, his team springs into action. This is how it is done: When the chief finds that the time is ripe, his troop approaches the lantern and the chief first gives the so-called preliminary command ("Attention!"), whereupon the deputy reaches for the long pole and waits. The chief commands "Lights on!", and with a skillful twist the deputy flicks the lever on top of the lamppost. During this operation the assistant lamplighter must always keep his equipment handy, for he is in charge of the technical work; he is the one who supervises the tools: hammer, pliers, drill, cable, spare carbons. All these are his responsibility.

The layman will have a hard time understanding the many technical terms used by lamplighters. If a street is completely illuminated, the condition is known as "full light." By no means does a lamplighter "ignite" a lamp—he "gives light"; toward morning the lamps are "de-lighted," the pertinent command being "De-light!" When the light-up levers are oiled, which is usually done toward the end of each month, an oilcan is used. The assistant lamplighter is in charge of this oilcan also.

With the exception of the technical assistants, the lamplighters undergo strictly scientific training. The requirements for this profession are stringent; a man who aspires to it must have first-class references, must come from a politically unexceptionable family, must have undergone voluntary military training in a Reichswehr unit, and must be a graduate of a secondary school. He receives his professional education at an institute of technology. For a future administrative official, participation in physical exercise (bending from the hip, muscular flexibility) is mandatory. The curriculum includes the following: The Nature and Concept of the Science of Light; History of Illumination, With Particular Reference to Regional Conditions; Theory of Lighting: On-Light and Off-Light; The Sociology of Photology. The course of studies is followed by a civil service examination. After a waiting period of ten to twelve years the candidate is usually appointed to the position of lamplighter; after another twenty to thirty years he is promoted (not appointed) to the rank of chief lamplighter.

It is easy to see that these are highly qualified old hands who perform their difficult tasks in rain and wind. In the half-century of their professional activity they have been able to gain universal respect and recognition. They are organized in the Reich Association of German Lamplighters (RAGL), with autonomous regional groups in Bavaria, North Thuringia, and Hamburg as well as in local chapters, the most important of which is the Streetlighters' Association Berlin (SAB).

The officials are continuously improving their knowledge of technology, demography, urban planning, and traffic development. This year, they finally managed to persuade the state universities to offer programs leading to the degree Dr.lux. The advanced training of the officials is provided at special lamplighter academies and seminars; the teachers are organized in the Reich Association of German Higher Lamplighter Education Instructors. Their work is not free from peril; during the laboratory sessions it may happen that an overheated lamp explodes, and therefore all instructors are insured. (For further details see the Journal of German Higher Lamplighter Education Instructors Insurance Associations.)

The present members of the guild of lucifactors, as they like to call themselves, are almost without exception from the better classes of society: Sixty-five percent of the chief lucifactors and forty-five percent of the deputies are former reserve officers. This alone guarantees their political reliability. In some families the love of light has, so to speak, become an heirloom; there are officials who practice the calling in the third or even the fourth generation. The majority of the assistant lamplighters are, of course, also ex-servicemen, since it is among this group that one is most likely to find the stolidity—to use the technical term—that is a sine qua non for the lucifactor profession.

The various branches of our government are greatly interested in the professional activities of the lucifactors. Thus, their recent Fifth National Light Congress was attended by His Excellency Lewald from the Reich Commission for Physical Exercise, though his other obligations relating to all the congresses held in Germany must keep him very busy. In an official proclamation, the Reich Defense Minister drew attention to the excellent service of the lamplighters and wished them the good old spirit of 1871. Now the lucifactors are also assured of being represented in the National Assembly; as you will recall, in a recent election Dr. Kick of the German People's Party (seat of Pantz) became a member of Parliament. He is a lucifactor who knows the trade from scratch and will safeguard the interests of his colleagues in a true streetlighter spirit. It is he who, together with a representative of the Reich Defense Ministry and Admiral Stenker of the Navy, inaugurated the Lamplighter War Memorial in recognition of the fact that the lamplighters have a large share in the casualties of the World War and thus have contributed a great deal to the recovery of the Fatherland. The men of light have entered literature as well; we need only mention Rudolf Herzog's novel *More Light*.

In Berlin's Darkinger Street rises the trim national headquarters of RAGL. After the recent great factional squabble, peace and order have been restored within the organization. At that time, the interests of the organization were represented by an attorney named Löwenstein—Jewish, but not very bright, and therefore national-istic. He has now been replaced by Dr. von Falkenhayn, a great-nephew of the well-known victor of Verdun.

Truly a veritable symbol of German strength and German dili-gence, German initiative and German loyalty: that little troop which, almost unnoticed, plods through the streets in the evening, plying its hard trade. There have been occasions, particularly in working class districts, when the officials were annoyed by Com-munist-incited adolescents shouting "Night Watchmen! Night Watchmen!," but the authorities sternly intervened. The police and the judges did their duty, and in each case the perpetrators were heavily fined for violating the Law for the Protection of the Repub-lic. German justice, in its traditional objectivity, demonstrated once again what it is capable of.

From the unobtrusive appearance of these simple men one can-not tell how much German activity resides in them and their work. Let us hope that they, aspiring to ever greater heights, will perform their services for the national welfare and for the benefit of the Ger-man state until, some day, times will be better and German light will also glow in Strasbourg, Danzig, Vienna, Budapest, and New York.

And so, in this spirit, "Good light!"

Street lamps can also be turned on from the central office.

Procreation

Zeugung, 1927

The biochemical process is well known.

This is how it looked on the outside: the bare, curtainless window turned first light-grey, then grey-blue; finally the sky became whitish. The woman was the first to awaken; in dirty panties, with her disheveled hair hanging down over her face, she looked around dully. The tangled disarray of the room greeted her. Through her gummy, squinting eyes she saw the following: the stove with pots and dishes; on the table, two empty bottles and a half full one; her petticoat on one chair; his things thrown over the back of another; boots, baskets, crumbs, dirty dishes, sheets of newspaper, a hammer. The less people own, the more cluttered their rooms are. This couple had only one room—kitchen, dining room, bedroom, and living room all in one, in it they had begotten a child the night before.

That it would turn out to be a son the woman didn't know yet. She looked at the man; he was sleeping with his mouth half open, badly shaven, sweaty around his nose. Her glances awakened him. "Make some coffee," he said in a low voice. She wanted to continue their caresses. He kissed her and gently pushed her away. She got up. He, the father, watched her from the bed as she busied herself with the pots.

The room looked like a coroner's inventory, like the photograph of a room in which a murder has been committed. The man sat up in bed and reached for his woolen underwear. Then he shuffled out into the corridor in his slippers, to the toilet.

The future mother put bread crusts and a knife on a corner of the table and two cups of coffee beside these. He came back and they ate. They did not talk. There was nothing to say. He chewed and looked out the window. There was the city. He looked past the chimneys on the roofs without seeing them. Because a man can look only into his past and not into his future, he saw nothing. Two courtyards away stood a horse, a young animal, which two years later was going to kick him in the belly; this would hospitalize him for months, out of work and sick. Around the corner a clerk was sitting in an office, sharpening his pencil; with this young, anaemic, pimply fellow the woman was to run off. Behind, far on the horizon, there lived a physician who would not be able to help him, and farther west there was the factory owner who was going to fire him later on. But for the time being the man stolidly chewed away.

The thing, which was inside the mother, that tiny seed, became a son. He was to perish at Verdun, on the same day on which General Falkenhayn got the order Pour le merite.

Mr. and Mrs. Parent got up.

An Embryo Speaks

Die Leibesfrucht spricht, 1931

They all take care of me: the church, the state, the physicians, the judges. I'm supposed to grow and to thrive; I'm supposed to slumber for nine months, to take it easy—they wish me well. They protect me and watch over me. Heaven help my parents if they do me any harm; then they all come running. Anyone who touches me is punished; my mother would land in jail, so would my father; the doctor who'd do it would have to stop being a doctor; the midwife who'd assist would be locked up. You see, I'm something precious. Yes, they all take care of me: the church, the state, the physicians, the judges.

For nine months.

But once these nine months are past, I'm on my own.

T.B.? There's no doctor to help me. Nothing to eat? No milk? There's no help from the state. Torment and mental anguish? The church consoles me but does not fill my stomach. And I haven't a thing to eat, so I go out and steal; immediately there's a judge who locks me up.

For fifty years of my life no one will look after me, not a soul. I'll have to shift for myself.

For nine months they kill one another if someone wants to kill me. Now I ask you: Isn't that a strange welfare system?

A Boy from My Class

Ein Kind aus meiner Klasse, 1925

The other day I met a boy from my class after all those years. It was about the way it is in picture books: the poor man stands outside by the fence, begging, while the well-to-do man inside brushes cake crumbs from his vest. "Don't you recognize me?" says the poor man softly. Then the rich man recognizes his former schoolmate and… I've forgotten how the story goes on. Anyway, the boy from my class with whom I used to stroll about in the old schoolyard, discussing the finer things of life, has since become a government councilor, and I suppose I won't amount to anything in this life. And I'm not so sure about the hereafter either.

So I talked over old times with this fellow. That's a wonderful kind of conversation, and there is only one book in which it is reported correctly: my favorite book, Philippe Monnier's Le Livre de Blaise.* It tells what happens when two people meet again; how one recognizes never the man but invariably only the boy; how the little school matters stick with one for life; how people basically remain the same; and how everything is predestined. What, then, is retained? Monnier: "Leveque is a Catholic." Period. That's all he knows about that fellow, and that's all he'll ever know.

I recognized him immediately; he was still the same refined, gentle, very superior, very pleasant person. We sat next to each other at the table, surrounded by terribly famous people, but I didn't see or hear a thing. I even passed up the ice cream twice. I was little again and went strolling through the schoolyard just as I had done then.

---

* Tucholsky cites the title of the German edition, *Blaise der Gymnasiast* (Blaise the High-School Student).- H.Z.

"Do you still remember... ? Can you still recall... ? That guy always had dirty hands and prompted beautifully." All our fellow students reappeared, and so did all our teachers, of course. And I almost asked, right in the middle of those fine people: "Have you done your geography? I don't know a thing!"

And when we had pulled them all to pieces—the teachers, the headmaster, the caretaker, and all the higher and lower grades—I had a bitter taste in my mouth. For that boy had said in his soft voice: "just think... it's too bad about all those lost years!" It was the death sentence on the German school system, a far harsher and more radical verdict than the noisiest political assembly could pronounce.

The lost years... . I remembered things that I hadn't thought about for decades—and now they suddenly were there again. No, they didn't beat us. Nor were things romantic; nobody shot himself when he had to repeat a grade, and there was no such thing as "Spring's Awakening." This awakening took place gently in each individual and was calmed down again in one way or another. Nor was there a pupil named Törless among us. But they did rob us of our time; the tuition was lost, and so were the years.

There were boring pedants everywhere, inadequate teachers, many errors—well, we weren't perfect either. But what did they teach us? What did we get out of it?

Nothing. We didn't even learn to think correctly, see correctly, walk correctly, work correctly—nothing, nothing, not a thing. We received neither a good classical nor a good practical education; we got nothing.

He said: "If we hadn't worked at home by ourselves! If we hadn't had a decent upbringing!" Well, I for one didn't receive one, and I envied him greatly. He said: "All I know about the history of art, political history, and European geography I taught myself." Who else should have taught him? Our school, maybe?

Our school wasn't as poisoned by nationalism as today's schools are. Our teachers weren't any more unintelligent, lazy, industrious, or clever than other teachers. It was a school a little below average, but not much. And what did we learn?

German: a ridiculous dismembering of the classics; fatuous essays, sloppily and injudiciously corrected; Middle High German poetry was learned by rote, and no one had an inkling of its beauty.

History: a senseless, incoherent compilation of dynastic dates. We never had history instruction.

Geography: tributaries. Government districts. Names of cities.

Latin: cramming. I have never been able to read a Latin writer. Greek: see Latin.

French: indescribable.

Natural Science: God knows what mischief went on there and in Physics class! Not one experiment went well—except. perhaps, the experiment of using wholly inadequate materials to give even more inadequate physics instruction.

Math: mediocre.

And so on. And so forth.

I don't think back to my schooling with hatred—it has become a matter of complete indifference to me. We never had any tragedies in school, nor terrible grievances. Bad teaching is what we did have.

Things were similar afterwards at the University—but there, at least, the professors' inability to teach was often compensated for by their scholarly worth. But it is with some sadness that I think back to school, now that I've learned to appreciate the value of time. They cheated us out of time, of our time and our youth. We had no teachers, we had no guides; we had officers of instruction, and not even good ones. I remember asking a friend after graduation: "Well, what about the tutors?" "Stupid, as always!" he said, and there was so much natural contempt in his voice—not even hatred.

I don't know nearly as much as I ought to. I am deficient in many things; I am not even equipped with an academically trained mind to apply to areas that are a little out of the way— and such a trained mind would be a lot. I have no equipment. What we know and what we can do, we had to take enormous pains to teach ourselves afterwards, when it was already too late, when our minds were no longer as receptive as before. Perhaps some things would have turned out better if we had gotten good instructions.

And they are so proud of their schools! How they crow when they hold their congresses of philologists; what great words, what pathos! Has anything changed? I don't know what Definite School Reform is, but I do know that what is being done today is definitely not school reform. It may well be that competent non-commissioned officers will be produced, or perhaps desperate men, but they will certainly not be educated men, instructed men, well informed men.

Before the war a man named Graf edited a book of reminiscences about schools in which a lot of well-known people of that time gave their recollections of school days. It was frightening how much hatred, revulsion, and contempt jumped out at one from these pages!

All we do is shrug our shoulders. But what if that boy from my class has a child of his own—what then? That child will have to be put in the same school, the same school for which no money is available—because, after all, we need five hundred million for our military budget—the same schools in which poor people are robbed of their time and about which rich people laugh. Of course, we warmed up the old anecdotes about teachers: the one about the purist who refused to use any foreign words and therefore wore a pinch-nose instead of a pince-nez; the one about the "sweet guy"; those about the "academic V.I.P." and all the other poor fools. All that is past history now. But we are left and so are the ill effects of this ridiculous school, which really wasn't any. If that boy from my class has turned out well, it happened in spite of our school, not because of it.

For the German schools of today have an ideal which must be described as the basest of all; their guiding thoughts, their ideas, their curricula are at the very bottom of all human development: they are militarized.

The Foreigner

Der Fremde, 1924

One day Frau Kulicke meets a Chinese on the stairs; she comes home quite excited and asks: "Is there a Chinese living in this house? On the stairs just now... ." The bell rings and she opens the door; it is the Chinese. For heaven's sake! What? The Chinese would like to rent a room. Somewhat suspiciously she lets him in; the Chinese looks at the room, likes it (he doesn't have that Berlin eye for such things yet—if I'd been there, I could have shown him a thing or two), he rents it, and moves in. He becomes an inexhaustible topic of conversation.

To Frau Kulicke, he represents China. In her mind she mulls over unsuspected possibilities—opium dens, pirates' braids torn off, little geishas (these are in Frau Kulicke's Chinese Department). But in the midst of this Asiatic cauldron, one thing is sure: China and this Chinese—they are one and the same thing.

And Frau Kulicke is only one among a hundred thousand. For most people, every foreigner represents his entire country, his government, his potentate. Until a short time ago, all the Frenchmen in Germany, as everybody knows, had special private assignments from Monsieur Poincare; before the war the Germans were emissaries of the Kaiser; on every Russian there used to be the reflection of the Tsar (whom he may never have seen). To most people, a foreigner represents his state. And nobody has the obvious idea that at home the foreigner might be as useless, pushed-around a thing as his host; that his state might bother with him as little as ours does with us. (Recently it said in a proclamation regarding the celebration of some constitution: "Segments of the population are to be invited to participate also.") Everybody still behaves as if a powerful constituent of a completely unified tribe were coming to us, and not a miserable component of an anachronistic form of society. And the more powerless the natives are, the greater the powers they believe the foreigner to possess.

Europe has never had as many nations and states as it does today. Within these states the game goes on—or do you suppose the Franconians will stand for the suppression of Middle Franconian individuality among them? "The Thuringian interests" (best pronounced like 'innerrests')... ; the inhabitants of the Palatinate demand... ; the Hanoverians threaten—half a million people each, at most. Europe is playing. This idea seems to be on the point of tilting over into its opposite—or let us hope so. Instead of seeing how class lines really run, they amuse themselves with flags, boundary lines, prime ministers, and play at "being foreigners."

God's blessing on this continent! It will need it.

Herr Wendriner Makes a Phone Call

Herr Wendriner telefoniert, 1922

*On the day of Walther Rathenau's funeral in 1922, all mainland telephone
service in Germany was suspended between 2:00 p.m. and 2:10 p.m.*

If he won't honor our invoice, I'll simply give him a buzz. Put
the envelopes on the chair for now. What's Skalitzer's exchange?
Königstadt? Just wait, boy, till I... What's that? Huh? What's the
matter? Operator! Why don't you answer? How do you like that—
she doesn't say why she doesn't answer. Operator! Doesn't the phone
work? Miss Tinschmann, whatsamatter with this phone? Is it out
of order? How often have I told you... ? What? What is it? Service
suspended? What's the meaning of this? Why... ? Oh, on account
of Rathenau. Thanks, you can go now.... On account of Rathenau. Very well. That's only fair. The man was a merchant prince,
our greatest statesman. Can't deny that. A disgrace they shot him.
A real decent person. Knew his old man well—that's what I call
merchants! Well, they had quite a memorial program for him in
the Reichstag. Most impressive. A terrific editorial this morning—
first-rate. Yes, the government is going to take some pretty strong
measures—it has already issued an order. Shooting him from a
car—outrageous! The police ought to ... Operator! Guess the ten
minutes aren't up yet. Must have been crack shots, those fellows.
Officers, maybe.... Can't really imagine that, though.... Had all
the boys from my son's regiment over for dinner that time, didn't
I? Such nice, high-class people. Terrific personalities, some of them.
I got a big kick out of it when the boy became a reserve officer.
Operator! The longest ten minutes I ever saw. Operator! If they're
on strike one minute more than ten, I've got a good mind to send
in a complaint. Operator! I've got to talk to old Skalitzer. A hell of

an idea to shut off the phone because of that. That won't bring him back. Let 'em spread out the taxes more fairly, that would be more in the spirit of the deceased. Operator! Who's going to shut off the phone when I'm gone? Nobody! Crazy idea to shut off the phone! How'm I supposed to get through to Skalitzer now? By the time I do, the old boy will be out to lunch. Scan'alous! Those people want more pay, that's all. What kind of trick is that, to shut off the phone right in front of your nose, in broad daylight. All sorts of things happened under the Kaiser, God knows—but I've never seen anything like this! It's an outrage! This is a public nuisance! Let 'em kill each other or not—but they've got to keep it out of our business! And another thing, a Jew shouldn't make such a spectacle of himself. That only stirs up anti-Semitism. Since the ninth of November we haven't had law and order in this country. Is it necessary to shut off the phones? Who's going to pay me damages if I don't reach Skalitzer? Operator! Just listen—they're having a demonstration outside. Look—red flags yet—just what l like! What are they singing? Operator! They'll carry on like this until there's another revolution! Operator! They can take the whole Republic and… . Operator! Operator! My political principles are… . Operator! It's about time! Operator! Give me Königstadt… !"

Herr Wendriner Gives a Dinner Party

Herr Wendriner hat Gesellschaft, 1925

Good-bye, madam! So long, Mr. Welsch! Have a good trip home, and good night! Bye!… Ugh.

What time is it? God, it's a quarter past one! The Mannheimers were going to leave at 12:30, so why did you ask them to stay some more? We've got to cork the red wine, it's still quite good. Whee, am I tired! Did you shut the hall door? Who's there? Oh, it's Marie. Well, Marie, how did you make out? Go close the door. I'm sure Gerolds didn't even tip two marks, that woman is so tight… Vera looked very good tonight, don't you think so? Except for her blackheads; I'm surprised the girl doesn't do anything about them. The keychain? Haven't seen it. You always misplace your keychain. Why don't you look on the night table in the salon. No, I haven't got it. How often do I have to… . Keep your things organized. By the way, I'm not going to invite Aunt Jenny to a dinner party any more. She stuffs herself something awful. These are your relatives! My relatives don't fress, they just go bankrupt. Got the keys? Oh, thank God. Just take care of your belongings! The roast hare was pretty good, wasn't it? The ice cream was a bit too soft; the maid will have to watch that. Marschall sure stuck me with that liqueur. He told me it was something special, just for me; that stuff wasn't fit to drink. Well, they must have liked it; the bottle's almost empty. Too bad. Where is my cigarette case? Hannah! Hannah! Have you seen my cigarette case? Where's my cigarette case? Someone prob'ly stole it. Sure, where else would it be? Just a minute ago I… don't make me nervous! Help me look for it. Such a fine case. Maybe somebody took it along by mistake… Oh, there it is. What are you wrapping up at this time of night? Have the maid do it tomorrow. Come to bed now. By the way, the Regierers seem to know about

Oscar; I overheard them telling Lotte at the table, "Old furniture is no dowry!" The nerve! Incidentally, did you ask Dr. Landsmann what you should do about your bronchitis? I would have done it without batting an eyelash; that's silly. What's the man a doctor for? I'm not going to invite Jack any more, I'm telling you; he tries to sell insurance to everybody. I don't want any business deals made in my house; you don't do business in a living room.

"By the way, I talked to Bräunling; he told me that Meyerhold won't take that bunch of shares I told you about. Now stop your wrapping; it's half past one. Got the paper? Fritz says T.W.'s article was awfully good today; I've got to read it. What are all those bottles doing in the toilet? Have them taken out. Now the maid's gone to bed. But you could really have told her to take the bottles out. Where am I supposed to sit now? Hannah! Where's the stock exchange report? It's not in the paper. How could you tell Paul that Meinicke is giving us a special rate? You know that he's going to run there tomorrow, and then Meinicke will give me hell! No, not you! Me! That's it. Then don't put the bottles there. Help me pick them up. The whole bathtub is green; those stains will never come out. Those dinner parties! They'll come out; don't make such a fuss. It must have cost at least two hundred marks, all together. No, I don't really want to be invited! Do I get my hard-earned money back that way? Besides, the Siegels never invite you back—one time a child is sick, then they don't have a maid; I'd like to have so many excuses some time! No more parties for the next two months! That's final. Come on now, I've got to get up early in the morning; hurry up and go to bed. I'll be up in a minute; I just want to read that article. Don't step into that. I'm glad that vacations are coming; I can't stand the sight of all of them any more. Well, at Garmisch we'll be left in peace. The Meyerholds will be there too; the Welschs are coming and so is old Regierer. Lotte may bring along Grete. This way at least we'll have someone to turn to down there. Hannah! Hannah! We're out of toilet paper again! That bunch even used up our toilet paper! Never mind, I'll use the newspaper… !"

Herr Wendriner Educates His Children

Herr Wendriner erzieht seine Kinder, 1925

You gonna have another beer too? You are? Waiter! Waiter, for Heaven's sake, I been calling you for a half hour—so hurry up and come 'ere! Two Pilseners! What do you want? Cake? You've eaten enough cake. Two beers, then. Or perhaps you'd better… well, all right. Boy, be quiet; I can't hear myself think. But you've already had cake.

"No? All right, no. Waiter—another piece of apple cake with whipped cream. You've no idea how this boy wears me out. Now, Max, go and play. Don't always listen in when grown-ups talk. He's going on ten. So, as I was saying, I come home and my wife shows me the letter. You know, you could have knocked me over with a feather. I says to my wife: Things can't go on like this. Take him out of school—take him into the business! Max, stop that! You're getting yourself dirty. Let the boy get a good taste of life! If his father works so hard, he can work, too. I'm telling you, sometimes it isn't easy. And yet the boy sees work all around him; I leave the house at nine in the morning, sometimes at half past eight, at eight, even earlier; I get home in the evening, dead tired. Max, take your fingers outa there, you're wearing your new suit! You know, the big boom that time, in January it was, then the liquidation—by the way: d'you think Fehrwaldt paid his debt? He did like hell! I've turned it over to my lawyer. That man's no good, believe me. Well, then, my oldest boy isn't here any more. Max, stop that! He started with… So listen: I sent him to Frankfurt, to S. & S.—you know those people, too?—and he started as an office boy. I figured it this way: well, m'boy, stand on your own two feet and let the winds blow about your nose a bit—Max, don't do that!—well, we'll see. My wife didn't like it at first—I think this sort of thing is very good for the boy, financially and intellectually. He reads a lot. Max, cut it out! I told him: Boy, get some physical exercise! All your buddies go out for sports—why don't you? I don't get a chance to go with him—would do me a lot of good, too, the doctor told me—but he's got so many opportunities in Berlin! Max, stop it! So what do you think the boy does? Gets in a scrape with a dame from some joint—a barmaid, or something like that! Max, what do you want now? No, stay here! Stay here, I said! Don't you hear me? Are you deaf? Come over here! Come here! C-o-m-e h-e-r-e! Whatsamatter? Look out! The boy's pulling at the tablecloth... ouch, all the coffee is on your pants! Coffee won't leave stains. You dumb-cluck. Why don't you come right away when you're called? Now you knocked over the coffee! Sit down! Now you won't go any place. Sit down! Right here! And not a sound outa you! How do you like that— goes and spills all the coffee! Here's a piece of candy. Now be quiet. Yes—he's always been a riot, When he was born I opened a savings account for him—do you think he thanked me for it? School—? He wouldn't hear of it! But theatre! Didn't miss an opening night, knew every Reinhardt cast, and then came the films... Aw, you know—that was overdoing it! So now he's got this—err—Max, go and see if the lights are on up front there! But hurry back! Goes off with this dame. Costs a helluvar lot of money, you can imagine! And there's been trouble at the office—had to take him outa there; now he's in Hamburg. Heck, I said to my wife: Why didn't the Lord give us two girls? Girls you raise up, put clothes on them, put 'em to bed at night, and in the end they get married. Give you no trouble. But these? Nothing but! Max! Max! What's keeping the boy? Max! Where've you been so long? Sit down here. That boy will be the death of me yet. I'm telling you. Come on, it's cold, let's go.

"I'm just asking myself one thing: this flightiness, this careless-ness, these bad manners—where did the boy get them from?"

Herr Wendriner Under the Dictatorship

Herr Wendriner steht unter der Diktatur, 1930

S hush!
Didn't I tell you not to talk so loud? There are storm troopers outside the cinema… can't you see? Get out now. How much is it? I guess it's not going to rain, it'll hold up. Come on in. And shut your mouth now! Oh, I beg your pardon… Be quiet now. Where are our seats… ? First row… wonderful. All right—put your coat down over there, now your… give it to me.

"Previews. That's only a preview. We've seen that one anyway— it's… Regierer! Say, that's a good one! What are you doing here? What, in the boxes? Oh, well, the upper crust. hee, hee.… Oh, on passes. No kidding? Say, Regierer has two extra tickets he couldn't use. Welsch is coming too. Let's join them in the box. Wait, we'll come and join you… here… take your coat for a second… . Ah! Here we can talk at least.

"That was the newsreel. Parade in Mecklenburg. Big crowd, huh? Plenty of militia in here—you know, it actually feels like something is missing when they're not around. It does. You get so used to them. Fine looking fellows, some of them. Hell, I think it's kind of nice, come to think of it. Isn't it, Hannah? There's something festive about it. Sure there is. Well, Regierer, what's with you? What do you say? We'll see? That's what I always say. You know, things don't look so bad to me. When did I see you last? Two months ago… in September… . Well, there you are. Remember what a panic that was? You can't help feeling relieved because it's over… now at least you know what's what. Some atmosphere we had then… my wife put me to bed for four days, that's how run-down I was. Who would have thunked? Here on the Kurfürstendamm there wasn't a sign of anything. Say, look—that's Gebühr, Otto Gebühr. They say he had an offer from France a while back; they wanted him to do Napoleon. He wouldn't do it. He says the only part he'll take is Dr. Goebbels or perhaps Frederick the Great. Good actor. Real big right now. Big time for me, too! I... I voted Staatspartei that time because somebody had to take responsibility... and the party had the right outlook. That's right. Did Welsch really vote Centre? Meshuggeh. I'll ask him later. Anyway, things aren't so bad. I've been talking to a businessman from Rome and he says, compared to Rome, this country is positively free. You've got your yellow pass, haven't you? Sure, we've got our yellow pass. Ten years? I've been living in Berlin for over twenty years, so they gave it to me right away. Intermission now. Shush! Say, take a look at that dark-skinned fellow down there! Some Polish Jew, I'll bet... lemme tell you something, with kikes like that there's a reason for anti-Semitism. Take a good look at him. Disgusting fellow. What surprises me is that he's still around; why don't they kick him out?... Well. I can't complain. On our street everything's in perfect order. We've got a very nice storm trooper on the corner, a real nice fellow. When I go to work in the morning, I slip him a cigarette—he salutes as soon as he sees me coming; salutes my wife too. What did they do to you? What is Regierer saying? They knocked his hat off? How'd that happen? Well, in that case, my good friend, you'd better raise your arm! The way I feel about it is, if that flag's our national symbol you've got to salute it. Shush! Powder keg? I guess so. Do you think I feel quite safe? Every morning my wife rings me up at the office to see if anything is wrong. So far nothing has happened. Say, that was good just now, did you see it? The fellow pretended to be blind when he's actually deaf. Well, lemme tell you something... you shouldn't speak his name out loud... I'll tell you. About this H.—even if he does come from Czechoslovakia—he sure knows the German mind. At any rate, we have order. That's one thing we've got. As long as you're a citizen and got your yellow pass, nothing happens to you... you're under the protection of the state... they're very logical about these things. One thing you've got to admit: they know how to put on a show. Fantastic! What? Like the other day on Wittenbergplatz. The way they came marching up with their flags and all that music. Under the Kaiser it was no bett.... Welsch! You're a little late! Half the picture is over. Sit over here. No, not on my hat! Sit on Regierer's hat… it's not so new.

"Nu, Welsch, what's what? Let's have a look… now I can see you better. You look fine. Say, is it true you voted Centre? Here come two from Security. Shush!… It is true that you voted Centre? Meshuggeh. Sure, the Centre did have Karewski on its list, but that's Jewish business. We… not so loud! Keep your voice down, that's all I ask. Don't get me into trouble—times are too serious for that. After all, they're perfectly right in expecting us to maintain a certain decorum in public. Perfectly right. It's starting again. That's Kortner—see, they let him act. I'm telling you, it's really not so bad. Don't you agree? Of course you do. Cute little number—take a look! We were just talking about H. With him at least you know he isn't going to break into your safe. With the Communists I don't know. Or rather… I know too damn well. Yes, right now they can't move a muscle; they're out flat. Serves them right, too. My dear Welsch, a politician's business is to be successful; otherwise he's no politician. The same goes for a businessman. That's realpolitik. Let one handle politics and the other the realities. Am I right?

"Newsreel again? Well, why not? Shush! When they're showing those pictures, you shouldn't talk. Let them have their fun—it's not so bad. Anyway, it's good camera work; the other day we saw him from quite close; he was standing there with his lieutenants… No! Goebbels is out… Didn't you know that? Yes, sure he's very popular. Maybe that's why. H. keeps his eyes open. Goebbels wanted to speak in the Wintergarten… but they wouldn't give him a permit.

"Today it was a little weaker. A little weaker. Why? With the stock exchange, it's no use asking. The stock exchange has a nose… don't ask why. Those fellows have a flair; when things go well they don't say a word and make money, and when things go wrong they drive everybody meshuggeh. Afterward they'll tell you they knew what was going to happen all along. Charming picture, take a look! Say, did you see that? Those French soldiers running in all directions…? No, that couldn't happen in Germany. What was I saying? Well, even if some people are beefing, if you ask me, the thing has its good side. How so? What do you mean? What has that got to do with the war?

What has the Young Plan* got to do with the war? Go on! Did we start the war? All we did was cheer. And when it was over we didn't have any butter. Aw, don't tell me. Since when does a nation have to pay for losing a war? It's bad enough we lost it; the other side won, let them pay for it! My dear Welsch... I have... I am... shush!

"I expected... my dear Welsch... I expected certain things just the same as you did. All right. And now that I see it isn't the way I expected, I've got to admit that this system has its good side too. I mean, it has its historical justification—go on! You can't deny that. It has its... that is, I mean, the city does look different. And the foreigners will be back soon enough, out of curiosity. You've got to hand it to them: those boys have something. I don't know what it is, but they sure have got it.

"That's the end. So let's go home. Oh yes... the Horst Wessel song first. What are you gonna do—you've got to take part in it. The English sing their national anthem after the theatre, too, so we Germans sing a different song.... Marschiern im Geist in unsern Reihen mit.... Oh well.

"Beg your pardon... tsk, tsk, tsk... it's raining. So, it's raining after all.

"Wait a while... maybe a taxi will come along. You wait under the marquee; I'll watch for a taxi. That's not a Sturmtruppführer, it's a Gauführer... .

"I know the insignia. Get out of the rain. When it rains you should take shelter. Do we have to get wet? Let other people get wet. Here comes a taxi.

"Shush! Get in."

---

* A plan devised by an international committee headed by the American financier Owen D. Young. Intended to reduce the reparations to be paid by Germany, it went into effect in 1929. - H.Z.

Kurt Tucholsky

The Creed of the Bourgeoisie

Die Glaubenssätze der Bourgeoisie, 1928

The bourgeoisie is not very edifying in any country. National characteristics can tone down specific qualities or accentuate them; it seems that precisely this range of income and property determines a mentality that makes people shallow and hardened, chauvinistic out of anxiety, heartless out of narrowness of horizon, and rude out of lack of imagination. In this respect a Belgian Philistine does not differ from an American Babbitt, a German Philistine is no different from his French counterpart. People, who make more than the bare necessities of life, but not enough to meet the demands they accepted without understanding them when they chose to be bourgeois, simply are that way.

From the various strata of the bourgeoisie there stand out diverse types, which should be viewed separately. Nobody can know or describe them all; in a single country they are so numerous that a lifetime does not suffice to describe even half of them. To be sure, that would not be an "assignment" for a writer who isn't a student, but it would be an assignment, all right; and as far as I am concerned, the paltry visions of well behaved lit'r'ry fellas interest me far less than reality described by someone in such a way that it is brought quite close to us.

The various strata of the bourgeoisie crystallize certain axioms of which their holders aren't always conscious. In many cases they lead dull lives, unaware of their own selves, just as, in general, the blind spots in people's thoughts are much, much greater than is commonly assumed. Such statements as "There is a God" and "The whale bears its young alive" don't make most people think. They learned these things in school and that is the way it has remained. The axioms I am talking about are articles of faith, of iron construction, accepted in absolute obedience, retaining validity for a lifetime. They haven't been the same at all times. The armor of prejudice with which a citizen of Bremen surrounded himself in 1874 was forged of different plates from that of a Bavarian secondary school principal of the year 1928. But they wear this armor until they die and never take it off. They have their vacuums; they divide the world very strictly into large and small print; what is distant gets blurred, and they never get out of the lowlands of their dim cognition. That is the way it has always been. But because nowadays they are ridden by the demon of arrogance who whispers in their ears that he who has technology needs no soul (and, besides, has got one already)—for that reason it is worthwhile selecting from the extensive herbarium two plants that I have pressed for myself. What is characteristic of a person is that which he considers a matter of course. Let us take a look.

Frau Emmi Pagel from Guben, Lower Lausitz. Wife of Paul Pagel, bookkeeper, who calls himself a "works official" on his papers. Frau Pagel is of medium height; her legs are a trifle too fat; she has wide hips, a fresh complexion, is well scrubbed but not well groomed; she has fat, manicured fingers, with a signet ring and an ornate wedding ring. Hair cut short. By no means a provincial woman, but just a woman who happens to live in a small town.

These are her ten articles of faith:

I. Under the Kaiser everything was better.

II. A head bookkeeper is more than a bookkeeper.

III. A letter mustn't start with "I…;" that is impolite.

IV. The Jews are to blame for all the misery. The Jews are dirty, greedy, materialistic, voluptuous, and swarthy. They all have such noses and want to become ministers, provided they aren't already.

V. Of course there are no ghosts. Still, it is uncanny to walk in a cemetery at night or to be in a big dark house alone (mice).

VI. Servants are a race apart from the propertied, but they don't feel it.

VII. If you put sugar in rhubarb, it turns sour (This item is quite senseless; it stems from a misunderstanding and thus is ineradicable).

VIII. Communism means that everything is chopped to bits. In Russia the women are raped; they murdered a million people there. The Communists want to take everything away from us.

IX. What everybody, including myself, likes is pretty; what everybody, excluding myself, likes is beautiful.

X. The whole world is against Germany—out of envy.

So much for Frau Pagel. On the other hand, Frau Margot Rosenthal, a lawyer's wife, is rather tall, a bit too skinny to be called slender, very well groomed, but doesn't always look that way. Her hair isn't oily, but you'd think so. As for her complexion… "You wouldn't believe all the things I've tried for my…"

I. Gentiles are less smart than Jews and that is why they are called "Goyim."

II. Of course there are no ghosts. Still, one doesn't have to go to a churchyard alone at night… I don't have to try everything.

III. Anyone who is able to buy and collect French engravings is cultured.

IV. Communism means that everything is chopped to bits. The Commies want to take away everything it has taken us such trouble to buy, piece by piece. Of course, we've got to have workers and one should treat them decently; the best thing is not to pay any attention to them.

V. The whole world is against the Jews—out of envy.

VI. Art must not be extreme.

VII. Someone who sits in an elegant hotel is elegant himself.

VIII. During a thunderstorm one must turn off the electricity (cf. Frau Pagel, VII: Rhubarb).

IX. You can't send any husband alone to Paris, least of all mine. An ounce of prevention…

X. My husband is too good-natured.

So much for Frau Rosenthal.

And who will press the other plants?

Part II
No More Wars

A forest by Ypres, Belgium, in World War I. Ypres was one of the major battlefields, and became a symbol for the war.

A Look into the Distant Future

Blick in ferne Zukunft, 1930

And when all is over, when all has run its course, this mass de-lusion, this delight in banding into hordes, yelling in hordes, and waving flags in groups; when this modern mania for turning human baseness into goodness by lying has passed; when people have become not smarter, but tired; when all fights against Fascism are over and the last libertarian emigrants have passed away—then one day it will again become very modern to be a liberal.

Someone will come along with a thundering discovery: he will discover the individual. He will say: "There is an organism called man, and he is the important thing. And the goal is his freedom. Groups are something secondary; the state is something secondary. The important thing is not that the state should live—it is that the individual should live."

The man who will say these things will make a big splash. People will hail his doctrine, saying: "Why, this is something brand new! What courage! We never heard this before! A new epoch of human-ity is dawning! What a genius we have among us! Forward! The new doctrine!"

And his books will be bought, or rather those of his imitators, for the first one is always the fool.

And then this will have an effect, and a hundred thousand black, brown, and red shirts will be thrown into a corner and on the rub-bish heap. And people will get the courage of their convictions again, without majority decisions and fear of the state that made them shut up like whipped dogs. And this is the way things will be, until one day…

The Border

Die Grenze, 1920

A wide expanse of landscape. Mountains, valleys, lakes. The trees rustle, the springs gush, the leaves bend in the wind.

Diagonally across a forest clearing, through the forest, over the highway, runs barbed wire: the border. On either side, men are standing. The men on one side wear blue uniforms with yellow buttons, and those on the other side wear red uniforms with black buttons. There they stand with their guns, some smoking, all with serious faces.

Yes, sir, that's the border. This is where the states meet—and each state very carefully sees to it that the inhabitants of the other do not pass over the boundary line. This blade of grass you may still crush, this brook you may still jump over, this path you may still cross. But then—halt! Not another step! This is the border line. One step forward and you are in another world. One step forward—and you may be punished for something you might do with impunity over here. One step forward—and you may revile the Pope. One step forward—and you have become pretty much of an outlaw, a "foreigner."

Shame on you, foreigner! You are the most miserable creature under the European sun. Foreigner! The ancient Greeks called foreigners "barbarians," but they did offer them hospitality. But you, the foreigner of modern times, are driven from place to place; here you are refused a visa and there you are denied a residence permit, here you must not consume any bacon and from there you must not export any—you foreigner, you!

And the thing they call Europe has become a multicolored patchwork, and a man is a foreigner if he so much as sticks his nose out of his village! There are more foreigners than natives on this divinely blessed continent.

After this war, after shifts compared with which the Great Migrations were a day's excursion, mere child's play, after bloody marches of the peoples through half of Europe, the parochial affairs of every little district have assumed a fiendish importance. The old boundaries of Graustark and the People's Republic of Bavaria and autonomous Upper Silesia and France and Congressional Poland—it's the same thing everywhere. Everybody thinks his shop is the most important and has no intention of yielding even one iota. First of all and to begin with, let's draw a line of demarcation. We'll detach ourselves. A boundary, that's what we need. For we are in a class by ourselves.

But there is one earth on which we foolish mortals live, one ground under our feet, one sky above us. Borders run crisscross through Europe. But nothing, neither borders nor soldiers, can separate men in the long run if they do not want to be kept apart.

Wouldn't we today split our sides laughing at someone who'd urge us with gushing pathos to break down the barriers between Berlin and Magdeburg? In just the same way people are some day going to laugh at an international pacifist, 1920 vintage, when the time has come. Let us all dedicate ourselves to making that time come sooner.

A Minor Incident

Kleine Begebenheit, 1921

The stocking-weaver and the farmer's son had climbed at night from one field ditch into another; they didn't really know why. They had been told that they ought to do so, told by gentlemen who knew how to read and write. In the other ditch they were stopped immediately, that very night, and because they had exotically colored clothes on, they were badly beaten and locked in a house. Afterwards there was a lawyer behind a table—how glad he was to be sitting there!—who wrote down what the stocking-weaver and the young farmer had to say. There also was an innkeeper who beat them when they didn't say enough. A visitor came to see them and told them they were going to be killed—and from that moment on they were guarded by two people, a stonecutter and a young man who had no trade as yet and was living with his parents.

It took twenty-four people to shoot these two. Eighty volunteered, and these eighty included married and single men, reticent and forward men, vigorous and weak men—ordinarily good people who harmed no one and who simply wanted to be on hand to see what it was like when someone was shot to death, and more: who wanted to do the shooting themselves. For it was permitted… A coal dealer was their commander.

On the morning of that day the sad procession appeared on the enormous snow-covered field south of the village. The farmer and the stocking-weaver marched in front, between two of those who had been selected from the eighty volunteers; a physician from a big city who hadn't seen that sort of thing before and was also eager to see it; and the coal dealer with his men. The two wore thin jackets and trembled with cold and fear of death. The procession came to a halt behind the sheds. The lawyer, who had come along, showed the two a piece of paper; but they shivered and didn't know how to read anyway. They were placed against small black posts. The coal dealer told his men to load their rifles. He said it very loudly, although he was standing right next to them. He wished his wife could see how he, normally a coal salesman, was permitted to shoot two people here. The shots rang out. The two dropped like empty bags. The doctor from the big city went up to them and took a close look at their wounds. Then they were covered with earth.

I forgot to say that everyone was disguised—the condemned as Serbian soldiers, the executioners as German ones.

The White Spots

Die Flecke, 1919

In Dorotheenstrasse in Berlin, there stands a building that was formerly the Military Academy. At a man's height is a granite border that runs around the house, slab after slab.

These slabs look peculiar: they have white spots; the brown granite is light in many places—what can it be?

White spots, is that what they are? They ought to be reddish ones.

This is where the German casualty lists were posted in the "great" years. This is where those terrible sheets of paper were posted, new ones almost every day, those endless lists with names, names, names... I own a copy of Number One of these documents; on it the military units are still carefully noted, there are few dead on this first list; Number One was very brief. I don't know how many more appeared after it—but there were well over a thousand. Name after name—and each time it meant that a human life had been snuffed out or that a human being was "missing," crossed out for the time being, or wounded, or maimed.

That's where they were posted, where these white spots are now. Hundreds of silent people crowded around them, people who had their dearest ones out there and who were trembling that they might read one name among all the thousands. What did they care about all the Müllers and Schulzes and Lehmanns who appeared on these lists! Let thousands upon thousands perish—as long as he wasn't among them. And it was on this mentality that the war battened. And it was because of this mentality that it could go on like this for four long years. Had we all risen—all as one man—who knows how long it would have lasted.

People have said that I don't know the way a German man can die; I know it well enough. But I also know how a German woman can weep—and I know how she weeps today, now that she slowly, excruciatingly slowly, realizes what her man has died for. What he has died for...

Am I rubbing salt on wounds? I should like to burn the celestial fire into wounds. I should like to cry out to the mourners: He died for nothing, for a madness, for nothing, nothing, nothing!

In the course of the years these white spots will gradually be washed away by the rain and disappear. But those other spots cannot be effaced. There are traces engraved on our hearts that will not go away. And each time I pass the Military Academy, with its brown granite and white spots, I silently say to myself: Promise it to yourself. Make a vow. Be active. Work. Tell the people. Liberate them from national madness, you, with your small power. You owe it to the dead. The white spots cry out. Do you hear them? They cry: No more wars!

Someone Visits Something with His Child

Jemand besucht etwas mit seinem Kind, 1925

The farmer said, 'First to the right, then left as far as the small house, and then straight ahead.' Wait a minute. Here is the mayor's office... that is... that wasn't around then... it never stood here. Oh yes, here's the highway. I know the way now.

"Now pay attention, son. Over there we were stationed—from that hill there to about here. No, things have changed tremendously—all these things weren't there. No, nothing was, nothing. This is where we were entrenched; then there was nothing for quite a stretch, that was No Man's Land—it belonged to no one—and then came the Germans. That's where they were, over there—their listening post was stationed here—no, wait a minute, it was over there—yes, just where the pond is now. Their trench started there. Now I recognize everything. We always had four days up front here, then three days of rest back there. Yes, rest, and then leave too; that's when you were born; and then I came here again. No, all the farmers were gone, there were only soldiers here. There were quite enough of us as it was. Come forward a bit; perhaps I can show you something. Tired? We were tired too, sometimes. Yes, even at night, silly. Especially at night. Do you think it stopped then? Oh, we could see all right; they lit flares. Yes, quite a few. Many were shot dead. See the black crosses up there? That's the military cemetery, that's where they all lie buried, all of them... Look, across the field the trench must have run, right here. And where this tree is now, that's where the others were stationed. In between? In between were just empty fields. Five times we went over the top, we made five attacks. And they ran across it too, the Germans. Everything always remained the way it had been. Over there—sure, on that very spot—were the officers' quarters; that's where the medics came from at night, and right here is where the biggest hits were made. And on that spot, right where I am throwing the pebble just now, that business with Blanchard happened.

"Remember his picture? It's on Daddy's desk at home. Yes, the man with the big beard and the funny cane. That was Blanchard. Son, if you only had known him—there was nobody like him. Smart and decent and a real buddy. A real buddy like your pal Rene. Blanchard—good afternoon, madam! You certainly are still quite steady on your feet! Oh yes, a very hot day—Blanchard had sentry duty. A sentry had to listen for the enemy's approach. A shrapnel shell came flying and a piece of iron must have hit him right in the belly. That happened at midnight. Son, don't squeeze my finger so hard, nobody here is going to hurt you. And he screamed; three nights and two days he went on living. He always kept calling for me, for me and for his mother. His voice became fainter and fainter. In the end he could only wave a bit, a little bit, with a strip of his bandage. We weren't able to go out and get him. No one was allowed to go out there; it would have been certain death. At that time the Germans were especially furious; I think they had just lost a battle. And so we had to leave Blanchard lying there the whole time. I wanted to put a bullet into him so he wouldn't have to suffer so much. But it was no good, he was lying in a hollow, and, anyway, I couldn't do it. He screamed so loud that they came over from the neighboring trenches to find out what was the matter. Right here is where it happened. Back there is where our sergeant fell, that time they scored the big hit that cost us two squads... I must have been standing right about here. No, no! That's just what it says in your school books. You needn't believe everything you read in history books—none of it is true. But this here—this is really true, my son..."

"What's the matter, Daddy? Why did you stop talking? Why don't you take your hand away from your eyes? Daddy!"

A Vision

Vision, 1924

This is July 28, and the Paris bus driver is sitting at the wheel and turning the long, heavy bus as though it were a little two-seater. It says "A X" on the front of the bus. I'm not sure it's the right one and ask the conductor. He answers me politely: No, I have to take another bus to the rue de Grenelle. I thank him.

That is today. And what would the conductor on this Paris bus have done with me if we had met during those years?

This conductor would have shot at me—out of fear, out of a sense of duty, by command. His driver, in order to catch me, would have crawled cautiously along the trenches, resting motionless on his belly every few minutes: he would have waited, and then, at the next bend, he would have lunged ahead and stuck his bayonet into my stomach, right where I'm carrying my pocket mirror now. The man in the Metro who just punched my ticket would have lowered his rifle contentedly after I had thrown up my arms over there and vanished behind the German dugout… In these years.

And as for me, I'd have been duty-bound to bring the barrel of my gun down on the head of my milkman if I had caught him then, that man who is nice enough to tell me all the news every morning: I'd have had to swipe my side arms over the face of my colleague on the Oeuvre and to see to it that lovely Madame Landrieu never got to see her husband again. In those years.

Such was my duty, and such was theirs.

But now we're all peaceful again, exchange a friendly "hello": our ministers pay calls on each other. They give me directions in the street, we shake hands, I pass the time of day with them, they accompany me to the theatre, and we converse amiably about all sorts of things. All except this one question. About this one vital question: whether tomorrow they'll be at one another's throats with knives again: whether tomorrow they'll throw grenades (detonating on impact) into one another's houses: whether they'll ask Professor Haber if he can't invent a new gas, one that will completely blind people, if possible. They don't discuss the chance that tomorrow all of them—bus drivers, Metro inspectors, university professors, and milkmen—will change into a raving, howling mob with only one wish, namely, to turn their colleagues an the other side into a stinking mass to rot away in the trenches. Will it start up again tomorrow? Will it?

The Steadfast Tin Soldier

Der standhafte Zinnsoldat, 1930

The Steadfast Tin Soldier—what is it? "Tin figures are the most outstanding instructional aids and pieces of realia." So some German association has got its fingers on the tin soldier. And there he lies.

"The Steadfast Tin Soldier. News of Interest to Tin Figure Fanciers. An Illustrated Monthly for Collectors of Tin Figures." What will they think of next! I take a periodical for gravediggers, but one devoted to tin soldiers… !

The thing starts with a "German Creed" by General Clausewitz, and I suppose now we needn't read any further. This tin soldier isn't of tin at all: it is made of the same lead of which bullets are cast. There is a real "war game" in the magazine too: the French are before Greifswald, the Second Riflemen's Division is being transported out of Wittstock at twelve o'clock—I would have suggested Timbuktu—in short, there rages on a small scale that spirit of "military valiance" which, on a large scale, would have the world believe it is only the evil enemies of Germany that produced such turmoil in the land.

And the things that are offered for sale here—"Terrain accessories: draw well, haystack, ditches, fences"—they've got everything. "Available soon: one Prussian captain on horseback; one French captain on horseback." Gentlemen, there's something missing: you don't have everything. Here's what's missing: one half-decayed corpse: same, without head; two French wounded, with intestines hanging out: one Prussian captain with raised pistol: four Prussian workers, two of them lying on the ground. Terrain accessories: one wall, against it six Prussian proletarians, blindfolded: one pile of corpses. Also, the prize of any collection: one officers' casino during the "great time": same, with officers under the tables.

Andersen: "And then the little boy took up the tin soldier and threw him into the stove. He did it without giving any particular reason. No doubt the little goblin in the snuffbox was to blame for it."

Be this the will of God!

One Who Enjoys Life

Ein Geniesser, 1930

T he fat man speaks:
   "We were marching from Suwalki to the pine forest in order to clear up the battleground. I wasn't a hero—too fat for that. And the marching was tough—all the while we spoke about literature and cold Pilsener. That's when I made a vow: Theobald, I said to myself, if you get out of this safe and sound, you're going to feather your nest. Word of honor (we soldiers always give ourselves our word of honor). All right; the marching came to an end. Suwalki remained exactly where it's always been, and the war was over.

"Well, I didn't feather my nest. And I'm still pretty good at marching. But one habit has stuck with me and you wouldn't believe how much pleasure I get out of it. You see, there's this frosty glass of water. When I drink it—you'll excuse me—I look at this little slanting water level and do a lot of thinking. This is what I think:

"Picture yourself on a steaming highway, with the company, with all the dust and heat and this heavy cloud of male odors over the ranks, your shirt sticks to your body, on your thighs you feel a charley horse kicking, your pack drags you down—and, my God, what does it all mean… let's have a glass of cold water now… but it just isn't true! Now here is a glass of cold water, and I don't simply drink it down, oh no, I savor its coolness, I let it gurgle down my throat, I drink it in with my gills, like a fish, I taste all the torments which I don't have to endure—I tell you, it's a great pleasure.

"And this is what I do in many of life's situations.

"Things are pretty modest with me, as you can see. But just consider all the things I don't have:

"I walk around, and there's no boss to tell me: "Naturally, if you don't get here on time in the morning, you have to work late in the evening." There's no doctor to tell me: "Well, come right in—let's do some cutting up! Nurse, the cocaine, please. Put your head back—more…" There's no woman to say to me: "Is that so? Well, well! And the letter from Hedy? I suppose there's nothing to that, either! No, absolutely nothing. And yesterday, when Fanny… do you think I didn't notice how you made goo-goo eyes at Fanny, and in my presence, too; you can't even wait for me to leave the room. You're an old wolf—you don't care at all who it is as long as she's…"

"There no consular official to tell me: "Come again tomorrow for the visa. You'll have to bring a vaccination certificate of your grandmother and a written affidavit that you don't intend to start a parrot farm in our country. And—do you yourself have any infectious diseases?… Or are you by any chance a Communist?" There's no deputy party chairman to inform me of his "philosophy". There's no capricious little wife to tell me that she isn't in the mood today or ever.

"Just consider all the things I don't have! I tell you, that's some enjoyment.

"A Stoic? Oh, go on. Marcus Aurelius? Do I look like a Roman emperor? No, it's not that sort of thing. I've simply learned one thing in the war:

"If you constantly realize how much misfortune there is in the world and that at a particular moment you are not participating in it, that moment tastes twice as good. I don't live on the heights of existence. And yet everyone would very much like to. And that's why I dig myself a little hole and look down into the yawning abyss… My private happiness."

At Last the Truth about Remarque

Endlich die Wahrheit über Remarque, 1929

For months the Berlin yellow press has been howling advertisements for a disgusting concoction by Erich Maria Remarque. As a matter of fact, its title, *All Quiet on the Western Front*, was stolen from the Army High Command (Mr. District Attorney?), and it describes war the way only typical shirkers could imagine it. The next issue of the *Süddeutsche Monatshefte* will once and for all reveal the truth about this traitor; the information has been checked by Professor Cossmann and thus is almost reliable. Through the good offices of the publishers of this monthly we are able to enlighten our readers in advance of publication. For a long time Erich Salomon Marcus—that's the name of this little Jew boy—was a minor caretaker (a so-called *shelatten-shames*) in the Jewish synagogue on Oranienstrasse in Berlin. This scion of Judah was born in Zinnentzitz, Silesia, where his father Abraham Markus owned a kosher butcher shop (notice anything?). The years during which Daddy Markus plied his noble trade there were marked by the disappearance of a striking number of Christian children from the vicinity. Of course, these were always found soon after their disappearance, but it was never [!—Ed.] established whether they were really the same children.

Erich Salomon Markus never had a mother. As is customary with Jewish families, two mothers are recorded on his birth certificate, a certain Sarah Bienstock and an unmarried [!!] Rosalie Himmelstoss (a name about which we shall have more to say later).

At the age of nine little Markus began his "service" at the above-mentioned synagogue. His duties were to light the candles, dust the Bibles, and (something very important for the evaluation of his later development) to hold the Jewish male babies during their circumcision. On such an occasion his carelessness is said to have caused the son of a well-known Berlin department store owner to be circumcised twice, which is why Markus was fired from his job at the synagogue.

For a time Salomon Markus was an unemployed drifter in Berlin; he tried to find employment in the theatre, and it is said that several times he played all the title roles in Brecht's play *Criminals*, a production by Max Reinhardt, a fellow member of the Jewish race. In addition, young Markus was active in Berlin as a candy dealer, a pimp, a dog barber, and an editor. Markus is a Freemason and a Jesuit.

Then the war came.

Markus went to the front—that is, he was assigned to the Mounted Supply Corps, but on account of an illness, which we will not specify here, he was unable to serve and was used behind the lines. Owing to an incomprehensible oversight of the military authorities Markus was employed as a clerk in the main headquarters of His Majesty the Crown Prince; thus he never saw the enemy even from a distance.

After the war he settled in Osnabrück as a ladies' dressmaker; subsequently he worked as an assistant brakeman for the Jewish hearse in Breslau and later moved to Hanover. Professor Cossmann does not say whether Markus knew the mass murderer Haarmann and possibly acted as his accomplice...

And this lousy crook dares to write a report for the yellow press that has falsehood written all over its face! Not only does he use his own mother's name (Himmelstoss) in his book in order to denigrate one of his superiors (Mr. District Attorney?), but he also accuses German soldiers of committing cruel acts of which they have never been capable, for the German soldier was known for painless hand-to-hand combat and humane drumfire. Salomon Markus, of course, is unaware of this fact. While his comrades at the front were marching toward Paris singing "Deutschland, Deutschland über alles" and expecting to occupy it, but unhappily found it occupied, the Jew Markus was living it up behind the lines. When the German troops left, eighty-four illegitimate children were found in the vicinity of the Crown Prince's headquarters alone—and who but Markus could have fathered those?

Thank God his book has not met with universal approval.

German women in particular know what is proper. We must be grateful to them for knowing the difference between heroic Germans and unheroic un-Germans; it is they who look up to Siegfried, Hagen & Co. and the other heroes of our genuinely German legends. At a recent evening gathering in Berlin we had occasion to note with pleasure and enthusiasm that a German woman wants to look up to a hero.

As was evident on that evening, a German woman cares less about her husband's life than about his heroic death. She is ready to die with him each and every time with the cry "I'm dying!" on her lips—even if she should have to marry ten times! It is, among other things, by the length of his sabre that one recognizes a man's character, and a German woman demands that her husband be ready at all times to defend his fatherland—and if it is not attacked, we shall see to it that it is attacked! [A true German sentiment!—Ed.] A noble-minded German woman, the wife of a higher official, recently told us: "For me there is nothing more beautiful in our marriage than the moment when I can button hubby's uniform or unbutton it. It's an indescribable feeling."

Salomon Markus, however, has been judged. Through the imperishable article in the *Süddeutsche Monatshefte* his work has been exposed for what it is: a black torch bought and paid for by our enemies and the Marxists which cannot hold water against the shining armor of German defensive strength!

Part III
Getting Down to Suitcases

At the Baltic Sea. This is a typical wicker beach chair.
It was a popular tourist destination in the 1920s.

How To Travel Wrong

Die Kunst, falsch zu reisen, 1929

> *Whom God would show the highest favor*
> *He sends into the—*
>   "Alice! Peter! Sonya! Put this bag up an the
>   luggage rack—no, not here, there! God, these
>   kids never are any help. Fritz, stop eating all
>   the sandwiches! You just had your lunch!"
> *He sends into the world to rove...*[*]

When you want to travel, demand everything of the place you go to: natural beauty, the comforts of a metropolis, old artistic treasures, low prices, the sea, the mountains—in other words, the Baltic Sea in front and Fifth Avenue in back. If all that isn't available, start complaining.

When you travel, for heaven's sake don't have any consideration for your fellow travellers; they would interpret it as weakness. You paid for it—all the others are travelling free of charge. Consider that it is of enormous importance whether you have a window seat or not. If someone should smoke in the no-smoking compartment, he must be criticized instantly and sharply; if the conductor doesn't happen to be around, take his place and be the Police, the State and Avenging Nemesis rolled into one. This will enhance your trip. Be unfriendly in general; this is the hallmark of a man.

The best thing to do is to order a hotel room and then go elsewhere. Don't bother to cancel the room; no need to get soft.

---

[*] The beginning of a well-known poem by Joseph von Eichendorff, which has become a folk song. – H.Z.

Once you have arrived at the hotel, register with all your titles…
If you don't have any… beg your pardon… I mean, if someone
has no title, he should invent one. Don't put down "Businessman,"
write "General Manager"; this is very elevating. Then go to your
room, banging doors all over the place. Whatever you do, don't tip
the chambermaid if you have asked her for a few little extras; tips
only corrupt the common people. Clean your dirty shoes with the
hand towel, smash a drinking glass (but don't tell anyone; the man-
agement has so many glasses!) and then set out for a walk through
the strange city.

In the strange town you must first of all want everything to
be as it is in your hometown; if the new city doesn't oblige, it is
no good. The people, then, must drive on the right side of the
street, have the same telephone as you, the same order on the
menu, and the same lavatories. As for the rest, only look at those
sights that are listed in Baedeker's guidebook. Mercilessly drive
your companions to see everything that has a star in the travel
guide; blindly pass everything else by, and above all: equip yourself properly. On walks through strange cities it is best to wear
short mountaineers' pants, a small green hat with a shaving brush
on top, heavy nailed boots (very suitable for museums), and a
rough-hewn walking stick. Ropes are to be used only in cities of
more than 500,000 inhabitants.

When your wife drops with fatigue, it's the right moment for
climbing up on a lookout tower or for ascending the town hall.
If you're away from home, you have to take in everything that the
strange places offer you. If in the end your eyes get blurred from all
the details, you can say full of pride: I made it!

Make out a budget before you start travelling, down to the last
penny, and, if possible, a hundred marks short; you can always
save that much. By haggling, I mean; that sort of thing makes you
popular and enlivens the trip. Better go a bit farther than your
pocketbook permits and save the difference by walking where it's
more pleasant to ride, by skimping on the tips, and by regarding
every stranger as a vulture. And never forget the cardinal rule of
every wholesome trip:

GET ANNOYED!

Discuss only the little everyday worries with your wife. Warm up all the trouble you had back home in the office; and never forget that you have an occupation.

When you take a trip, the first thing you must do after you arrive in a strange place is to write picture postcards. You don't have to order these; the waiter will see that you want some. Write illegibly—that is a sign that you are in good spirits. Write postcards everywhere—on the train, in the stalactite cave, on mountain peaks, and in a rocking boat. In doing so, break the pencil point and spill the ink. Then start swearing.

The fundamental law of every real trip is this: Something has to be going on—and you've got to have a "plan." Otherwise the trip isn't a trip. Any relaxation from your work consists in your making detailed plans, but then not sticking to them. If you've failed to stick to them, put the blame on your wife.

Demand rural quiet everywhere. If you find it, complain that nothing is going on. A decent summer resort consists of an accumulation of the same people you see at home, plus a mountain bar, dancing by the ocean, and a wine cellar. Visit these, but stick to your proven costume: short pants, little hat (see above). Then look around the room and say:

"Well things aren't exactly elegant here!" If the others are wearing evening clothes, better say: "How snobbish to take along a dinner jacket on a trip!" If you are wearing formal dress and the others aren't start a fight with your wife. Have fights with her as a matter of principle.

Whiz through the strange towns and villages. If you're not panting for breath, you haven't planned things right. Besides, the train you've got to make is more important than a quiet hour in the evening. Such restful hours are nonsense; you don't go travelling for that.

On a trip everything must be a bit better than it is at home. Make the waiter take back the poorly chilled bottle of wine and have your facial expression say: "If my chief butler brought me a bottle from the cellar like that, he'd be fired!" Always act as though you were to the manner born...

You should by all means involve the ridiculous natives in an immediate discussion of politics, religion, and the war. Don't hold back your opinion; speak out freely! Give it to them! Speak loudly so they can hear you; a lot of foreigners are hard of hearing, anyway. When you are amused, laugh—and so loud as to annoy those stupid other people who don't know what you are laughing about. If you don't speak foreign languages very well, then shout; this will make them understand you better.

Don't become impressed.

If you travel with several men, it will be nice if at elevated places with a view you sing something like a barbershop quartet. Nature likes that.

Haggle. Complain. Get annoyed. And make a fuss.

HOW TO TRAVEL RIGHT

Work out your itinerary in a general way; let the motley moods of the hour fill in the details.

The greatest sight of all is the world; take a look at it.

Today no one has such a perfect picture of the world that he can understand and appreciate everything; be brave enough to admit that you don't know anything about a certain subject.

Don't attach so much importance to the little tribulations of a trip.

If you should ever be stuck at an intermediate stop, be glad that you're alive, watch the chickens and the serious-looking goats, and have a little chat with the man in the cigar store.

Relax. Let go of the steering wheel. Amble through the world. It is so beautiful. Surrender to it, and it will surrender to you.

Unpacking Your Suitcase

Koffer auspacken, 1927

Unpacking your suitcase in some strange place, the bag that has arrived a bit late because it stopped and had a little chat with other bags in transit—that's a rather peculiar thing.

You've already got acclimatized a bit: the doorknob has gently warmed to your touch; the cafe downstairs is already beginning to be your cafe; already little habits have formed. And then your suitcase arrives. You open it up... and a wave of home surges toward you.

There's the rustling of a newspaper, and suddenly you're again faced with everything you wanted to escape from. There is no escape. A shoe peeks out, and handkerchiefs; they bring it all back to you. They're so familiar to you it's almost painful. Are you ashamed of them? They are like too-close relatives you bump into at a party of strangers. Everybody calls you by your last name, but they address you familiarly by your nickname, and if you talk to another woman they wag a roguish forefinger at you. A fellow doesn't like that sort of thing.

Who packed that bag? Did she? A wave of warmth wells up in your heart. So much love, so much solicitude, such a lot of care and trouble! Did you thank her for it? If she were here now... But she isn't. And when she does come, you won't thank her.

The things in the suitcase don't speak the language of the country or of the town you're in. Their mute orderliness, their matter-of-fact cleanness in these narrow confines stem from that other place. There they lie, eloquent in their silence. With your eyes a bit out of focus you stand there in your hotel room and don't remember... no, you aren't even all there; you are where these things have come from, breathing the old air and hearing the old, familiar noises... At that moment you are living two lives: a physical one, this one here, which is unreal; and a psychic life, which is quite real.

Imagine a man who hangs his trousers in a closet lyrically! You ought to be ashamed of yourself! If a bachelor does it, it might pass. With sure, practiced hands he stacks things and puts them away, smoothing a bit here and brushing a bit there… But with a married man it is always somewhat ridiculous; he is like a baby in swaddling clothes who is suddenly given his independence—without his Mummy, a bit alone in the wide world.

That dressing gown doesn't just contain a memory; within its folds lie elements of that other world from which you've come. That's simply the way it is. But if you unfold it, those pieces fall out and evaporate; all of a sudden it hangs there, familiar and yet strange, like any old dressing gown that doesn't really care very much about the whole thing… And here there is something neatly rolled up; you can see a special packing trick here; did you stroke those neckties, old boy? As if you'd never taken a trip before!

You stand there in the room, slightly confused, with a shoe-tree in one hand, two pairs of socks in the other, and stare into space. A good thing no one can see you. All about you there is the rustling of trees, a bit of noise, the singing of three canaries, and the strange life around you has an intensity such as you never experienced in that other place. Drops are yielded by a sponge, which you never, never squeezed properly. Did it contain that much liquid? Weren't you aware of it? You took too much for granted, you were ungrateful. You know that now, when it is too late.

A bottle of cologne is broken: your good sheet has a greenish spot; there's an odor, and now your nose remembers. It has the best memory of all! People, beach scenes, songs, verses that you never thought about any more suddenly are back, full of life—hello there! Hello there, you say in surprise, drinking in the old smells once more. But after this first flash of remembrance there isn't much any more, for what doesn't come back immediately never returns again. A pity about the cologne, incidentally. The bottle has an ugly, jagged hole at the bottom; it almost makes it look like something from which life has oozed out… Oh, but that's a stupid superstition: it's no more and no less than a broken bottle.

Down at the bottom of the suitcase there are a few odds and ends, the crumbs of travelling, the stardust of distant places. Now your bag is empty. And there they are, your things, lying around on the chairs and on the bed, and now you finally put them away. Now the room is full and saturated, it's almost a little home, and all your memories are blown away, scattered, gone. A little while longer and you'll be at your next stop, yearning for this room, this stupid old hotel room.

Yousana-Wo-Bi-Rabidabi-De?

Yousana-wo-bi-räbidäbi-de?, 1928

Foreign languages are beautiful—if you don't understand them. I once asked the Danish writer J.V. Jensen how he managed to bring Asia so close to us—for example, in his *Exotic Tales*—and whether he had spent much time studying Chinese. "I like to travel in China," said Jensen, "because people there don't disturb me with their speech. I don't understand a word of it." That man is so right.

Foreign words are beautiful—if you don't understand them. A Babel of savage syllables is flying around your ears, and at any particular moment, God alone (as well as whoever utters these syllables) may know what is going on. How soothing to the nerves it is if one doesn't know what people want! "Where would it get you," said the wisest man of the century once, "if you listened to what the other fellow was saying?" In a foreign country it's all right to listen; it doesn't cost you anything. With your head inclined politely, you let your conversation partner finish—how seldom that happens in this world! And after he's talked himself out, you say, with a vague movement of your hand: "Me—sorry—deaf and dumb—no understand word—what you saying?" That's always pretty, and good for your health, too.

It starts at the border where the customs man says a lot of things, half of which are probably unpleasant; but they don't penetrate to your brain. As the Paris actress Maud Loti once said to her director at a rehearsal, they go in one ear and out the—yes, I think it was "out the other ear," but I may be wrong. And if the customs Charlie doesn't happen to have had a fight with his wife, it's possible that he'll leave you alone. After all, idiocy is stronger than all reason.

Now it happens all over the world that people, if you don't understand them, will speak good and loud with you; they think that an excess of vox humana on their part can replace the lack of vocabulary on yours. And if you're smart, you'll let them shout.

It's nice to be travelling in a foreign country and to be able to say in foreignese only things like "please," "thank you." and "registered mail." Usually the only words you know are the ones you don't get to use on the whole trip. That business with the dictionary and the phrase book I gave up long ago. You see, if you say one of those sentences to a stranger, it is as if you had stuck a pin into him—the torrent of foreign language simply gushes out of him, and none of it is in your phrase book… But how sweet it is not to understand anything!

Are you wondering what people are saying? Well, what do you suppose they could be saying?

You're missing the conversation of two men about the very important matter of the controlling shares in the safety-match trust; and then there's a shady real estate deal; and then a dirty joke (positively ancient!); and then they say good things about a woman neither of them wants and bad things about one neither of them can have—you needn't understand any of that. The little huckster at the station yells something that probably even the natives don't understand, and you can see for yourself that he's selling fruit of mediocre quality. You are gently woolgathering, wondering what on earth all these confused, incapsulated, rolling, rushing, half swallowed sounds may mean. These people must have different larynxes, different noses, different vocal cords; it's like in a fairy tale, and what you've learned in school doesn't help you, because the others learned it either wrong or not at all; and isn't it pleasant to knock about the world like a harmless fool… ?

"Well, I beg your pardon! When I go on a trip I want to know exactly what's going on; an educated person must at least understand something!" There certainly are differences in human life…

Staggering about in the labyrinth of language—well, it could be worse. "*Lon be fonteur ren main*," nasalize the Frenchmen. "*Normi baceffo della sornina*," vocalize the Italians. Let them nasalize, let them vocalize. I'm just wondering what foreigners may hear in Germany, with their ears, when our railroad porters, policemen, and hotel clerks say something to them in German.

It's a wee bit uncanny to speak with people without really communicating with them. That's when you first notice what an eminently pacifist thing language is; when it isn't functioning, primitive man awakens within us, the savage who is slumbering in the deep; a slight cloud of fear moves past, fear and then a touch of hatred: Who is he anyway? A stranger? What does he want here? And even if he has some business being here, what's in it for me? And especially on the street, in front of people who don't deal with foreigners every day, you feel a little like a wolf coming into a tropical forest—Wooo, howling under the tall trees, the wanderer takes a better grip on his club—and only if all goes well do they wave their arms in sign language.

But other than that, it's nice to wander through a world that doesn't understand us and that we don't understand—a world whose sounds reach our ears only in the form of "Yousana-wo-bi-rabidabi-de." Misunderstandings cannot arise because the common base is lacking—it is a clean, thoroughly honest situation. For how do people talk to people? Past one another.

The Flea

Der Floh, 1932

In the Departement du Gard—that's right, where Nimes is, and the Pont du Gard, in Southern France—there once was an old maid who worked as a clerk in the post office. She had a bad habit: she would open letters a little bit and read them. Everybody knew about it, but you know how it is in France: the concierge, the telephone, and the post office—these are sacred cows and you could meddle with them, but you mustn't—which is why no one does.

So the old maid read the letters and caused people a lot of grief with her indiscretion.

In this Departement, there lived a smart count in his pretty castle. Counts are smart, sometimes, in France. And this count one day did as follows.

He asked a bailiff to come to his castle, and in his presence wrote this letter to a friend:

> Dear Friend,
> Since I know that our postal clerk Emilie Dupont keeps opening our letters and reading them because she is bursting with curiosity,
> I am enclosing a live flea in order to cook her goose.
> Many kind regards, Count Koks

He sealed this letter in the presence of the bailiff, but he didn't enclose a flea.

When the letter arrived, there was a flea inside.

Kurt Tucholsky

Back from Vacation

Vom Urlaub zurück, 1931

When someone is back from his vacation, he may already be there, but he really isn't all there yet. "Well, how was it?" ask the others. "You certainly look rested! Did you have good weather?" So the fellow starts telling them. But if he has any ears at all he will notice that the question was really of the social kind; the others don't care for all the details. So he soon cuts his story short, if only because down here no one would understand why that one mountain simply couldn't be climbed, and as for Miss Glienicke and the goats, something that brought the house down back there, these people know nothing about that. How could they be expected to?

When someone is back from his vacation, he really isn't part of things the first two days. While he was away there were so many little happenings that of course he doesn't know about, and so there are a lot of allusions that escape him; he doesn't know that Bader is no longer in Department 3B but in the Finance Department, because he has had a fight with Koch, and they will probably throw him out there too. All these things the vacationer doesn't know, not yet or not any more, so he is briefed with a touch of pity. The tenor of those who have stayed at home is a bit like the tone, which "old experienced officials" usually employ toward a novice. The first two days, office life passes the ex-vacationer by; the others know everything, he only knows half. It's those people's ball game—he doesn't catch any of the balls.

His conversation still sparkles, willy-nilly, with his vacation. At one point he thinks: A week ago today... But then the phone rings and the memory goes up in smoke. Then a fellow comes along and asks the usual questions, and the answer is: "Thanks... but it was much too short. So... you're going on vacation too?" But that doesn't interest the ex-vacationer any more.

These first days, work really isn't any easier than it was before the vacation; if anything, it drags a bit more. Your lungs are still full of fresh air, your body still has some of the rhythm of swimming and running, your skin still feels strange under city clothes, and your neck doesn't like the collar. Your eyes look out into the yard; if you turn your head, you can see a little piece of blue sky. Incidentally, it isn't blue today, because it is raining. But rain in the country—that was something quite different.

Is the job still secure? It is. But no sooner do you go on vacation than they start to do foolish things. (Theme song: "Without me the whole business goes to pot!") Oh, it was a lot of fun in Giantville on the Shipashawnee; the trees rustled, we played gin rummy on the veranda, but during all that time those people here... "Mueller! Where are those papers?" Starting today this mess will be cleared up; WE are back.

This takes all of three days, maybe four. Then the others have got used to the returnee; he is part of things again, he is there, he shares in everything. Nothing welds people together so much as common working experience. It comes right after love and—heaven help us—the relatives.

After six days not a soul asks him about his vacation anymore. Soon the last vacationers return; everybody is back, and very slowly they all start looking forward to next year's vacation.

The Whispering Sanatorium

Das flüsternde Sanatorium, 1928

They have forbidden me everything: fat and goose butter and calf's greaves and sugar and bread and soup and wine and eel and all. My food is served in little birdseed boxes, and when I get my massage in the morning, I always exhale so as to seem lighter. Soon there will be nothing left of me; then I'll be weighing minus three pounds and they'll have to give me a refund when I leave the sanatorium… They have forbidden me everything. I live on air, music, and love.

The breezes blow gently on the magic hill. Love I mustn't talk about, because the little brunette is at present hitched to a prizefighter; but music I have brought along in a phonograph. This afternoon the new records I ordered arrived. Let's give a listen.

Right on top there's "Lindbergh's Reception in New York," something utterly asinine. Then there is Jack Hylton. And then "Miss Annabelle Lee," whispered by Mr. Jack Smith, the whisperer-in-chief, accompanied by a whispering orchestra. "Baritone, 78 RPM," it says on the label. The orchestra sounds like someone plucking a well-tuned rubber band; then that crooner caresses you with his voice. Incidentally, it's a quarter to nine, and in this rattle trap one isn't allowed to play music this late. But the record is so nice—I'd like to play it over and over again. What to do?

I stuff my imitation silk underwear plus two towels into the phonograph and turn it on; all you can hear now is a whisper not unlike the sound of a sewing machine. Miss Annabelle Lee! "…pretty little baby…" A King Louis of the phonograph is bending over the machine in royal solitude and has them play something for him. No nurse can hear me, no head nurse, no assistant physician, no senior physician, no medical director… Miss Annabelle Lee! What is this hush-hush music reminiscent of? It reminds me of the Berlin night clubs during the inflationary period when the touts, first looking around on all sides like conspirators, used to lead you secretly, stealthily, silently to a four room apartment on Bavarian Square where things were really swinging, whoopee! Naked floozies were dancing around the busily rising dollar over sugared champagne and roast potatoes. And everything was in a whisper; the girls whispered and so did the fat hostess, who was risking the confiscation of her apartment. The phonograph or the muted fiddles whispered and so did the guests and the waiters—what a discreet entertainment! That's how this music sounds.

And suddenly the whispering spreads to the whole sanatorium; it is contagious, everybody whispers… "*Leise, leise, fromme Weise…*"

There is whispering by the well rubbed bellies which in the morning resound under the blows of the murderous masseur; whispering by the patients, the overfed men and the hollow women; whispering by hysteria, hypochondria, and spurious health. The redhead in the garden whispers, "Do I look like that kind of a girl?" And one would like to whisper back, "Yes, my dear, you do!" There is whispering by Nurse Gertrude and Nurse Eliza, by the unmistakably Saxonian barber, and by the gossip with the eyeglasses. There is whispering by the old privy councilor who has been turned on by a young blonde; it may be his last fling, and he wears his hat at a rakish angle and walks around with jaunty steps, not considering what might happen if she said yes. There is whispering by the books in the sanatorium library, where Oncken's *History of the World* in twenty-six volumes whispers its world-historical lies. There is whispering by the patients in the radiotherapy area where the ultra-violet rays make everyone look like a powdered corpse; chairmen of the board and shrewd lawyers walk around there dressed in nothing but their dignity and dark glasses, which isn't much. There is whispering by Jumbo, the sanatorium's dachshund, who is against all inmates on general principles (and justifiably so). Only two lovers, who scarcely looked and yet found each other immediately, are no longer whispering; they are gasping their lives away.

There is whispering by the sour wife who keeps mentally counting all her possessions and is angry with people who don't envy her. There is whispering by the thermal water which, like it or not, has to lave the fat limbs of the corporation lawyers. There is whispering by the swing in the solarium, whispering in the shower room, whispering by the smart medical director (who should be played in the movies by Lew Ayres), whispering in the office, in the nurses' quarters, by the faithful head nurse (who reminds you of the sergeant of a troop of mercenaries), by the caretaker, who is counting the bottles of bootleg beer he has left. The watery ribbon of the Elbe flashes up, light-studded Dresden sparkles and gleams, and the winds whisper in the Saxonian dialect—in short, the whole sanatorium whispers.

And this with her singing
The Lore-lee has done.

Hark, the sound of a gang!

It's noon again, on the next day; life in the metabolism factory runs its accustomed course; now and again we gain weight and off and on we take it off; we are weighed mene mene tekel, weighed in the balance and found not wanting—Miss Annabelle, Annabelle Lee!

Crossward Puzzle by Force

Kreuzworträtsel mit Gewalt, 1930

The doctor burrowed in my abdomen. Then he got up and took a deep breath. "A case of nerves, Mr. Panter," he said. "Nothing wrong organically. Rest, relaxation, massage, fresh fruit and vegetables, exercise, carbonated baths… just wait, we'll get you back on your feet all right. Nurse… !"

There I was, in the booby hatch, and now it was too late. One should never listen to the advice of good friends. Nice prospects indeed!

Very nice. Every day I went through an extensive circus program from seven in the morning till twelve-thirty at noon. The physical instructor, the weight nurse, the bath attendant, the masseur, the intern, the regular nurse… they all worked so hard on me that I felt really sick, and when I felt sick they gave me a good dressing down: was I out of my mind, I was really doing much, much better. So what was I going to do?

Above all, what was I to do on those endless afternoons that were some eight or nine times as long as the activity-laden mornings?

Read.

The saladorium—never write "sanatorium"—the saladorium had a library. That was fine during the first week, for they had the General Almanac of Entertainment and Knowledge, a sort of family-type periodical from the Gay Nineties—what a tranquillizer! There was a story about a new, terrifying invention, the telephone, and another one about a vehicle called an "automobile" that could move by itself with the aid of a motor. At the beginning there was an illustrated novel: "Agatha caressed the defoliated rose and even the kind words of Councilor von Waldern could not console her (continued on page 95)." Then there was a detective story about atrociously dressed criminals—yet Edgar Wallace made the police constables of Scotland Yard much more villainous. And finally it had the "Miscellany," a charming mixture of trivia, recipes, pointless anecdotes, and blessed idiocy. This occupied me for a full week. Then it was finished. The remainder of the library consisted of more genteel literature, but what little I need of that I prefer to write myself. Now what?

One day, in the bathhouse, I noticed on the windowsill a puzzle magazine belonging to the attendant. I had never known that such a thing existed, but it did. It contained puzzles that could be solved by combining syllables from a given list, as well as other nice pastimes.

"May I... could you perhaps lend me this?" I asked. He lent. No sooner had I finished my fruit-and-nut cereal and the salad and that half plum than I hurried to my room, sharpened my pencil, and started to do crossword puzzles.

There are lots of gaps in my education. I have no idea where Karakorum is located; I don't know what "ephelides" are; I always confuse "phenomenology" with "pharmaceutics," and it is all quite hopeless. But I started solving.

At first it went quite well. Anything I knew right off I wrote into the little squares, and when I got stuck I would leave the puzzle unfinished and turn to the next one. I spent many fun afternoons that way. The tip-happy bath attendant brought me eighteen more puzzle magazines, but as if to spite me, they had no connection with one another, for the solutions of the puzzles I was nibbling on always were in the missing issues... Thus I had to try to finish everything by myself and was entirely on my own. I don't like that; whoever has counted on me has always counted himself out. But I solved.

When I had filled up those magazines, I had completed five crossword puzzles. All the others—and there were a large number of them—contained ominous white spots. What now?

Now I first bit my pencil to pieces, then one of the pens belonging to the saladorium, then my pipe. And I had ants in my pants...

Are you acquainted with the so-called Lahman syndrome? It's like this: after the patients have eaten pap for a while, they get terribly angry. They are in a frenzy from seven in the morning to eight at night, and especially toward late afternoon, when the very thought of cauliflower or even a good minute steak makes them hysterical. Then they start to rage in secret. They dare not do so in the open.

I did not dare either. But I raged with the crossword puzzles, determined not to let them get the better of me, and I decided to put a stop to it, one way or another. I couldn't go on like that.

"Mountain peak in the Maritime Alps." Now, I ask you—the Maritime Alps, of all places! Do you know where they are? I don't. I was absent when we took them up in school, or I may have been busy reading some popular novel under my desk. Maritime Alps! I had all the rows around it, but I lacked those letters that could not be guessed from the other rows. At that point I started cracking the crossword puzzles—with a sledge hammer.

KIKAM, I wrote. Mountain peak in the Maritime Alps: KIKAM. I found that very pretty. And this delighted me so much that I solved twenty-two crossword puzzles in one afternoon. By force. If they don't go willingly, get tough. I obtained wonderful results.

LEBSCH: a European capital. Don't say it—why shouldn't one of the many, many capitals of Europe be named LEBSCH? MOREL: light white wine. NEPZUSE: a planet. (No, not Neptune; that wouldn't work). Commercial term: INSOLENSKY. Friendly greeting: ROWDY. A predatory animal: TURDBIRD; yes, that's the way it came out—a word you once spoke you cannot revoke. And there emerged positively exotic words: MIPPEL and FLUNZ and BAKIKEKE. In this way I built a completely new world for myself.

I didn't tell anyone about it, but privately learned a new language: Crosswordpuzzlese. Had I mentioned it to anyone, they would never have released me from the booby hatch and I would still be there. But with those words shuttling back and forth in my mind I spoke Puzzlese all day and tested myself and already knew it quite well.

"Well, how do you feel now?" asked Uncle Chiefphysician in his, shall we say, kindly way. I did not answer immediately, for I was inaudibly practicing my vocabulary:

A flo was buzzing around the doctor's mesk; the xun was shining through the window and the sky was glear. I tried hard to recall the name of the part of my anatomy that I had reduced so nicely.

"How do you feel?" repeated the good doctor, mildly irritated.

"Thanks... much better," I stammered. What was that anatomical term? "Much better... yes..." "But a little absent-minded at times... still a bit nervous?" he asked, looking at me inquisitively. "Not at all, doctor," I said. "Not at all. I feel so refreshed! Really great! You helped me a great deal, a great deal!" "Oh, I'm glad," he said. "See—what did I tell you?" And in parting he gave me some bits of good advice, but unfortunately not the one to let his bill go unpaid.

And only when I was standing outside the gate of the saladorium did it occur to me. I wanted to go back and tell the doctor... but I didn't.

That part of my anatomy was the ASP.

National Notes

From Nationales and Schnipsel, 1924–1932

This continent is proud of itself, and it has a right to be. What people in Europe are proud of:

Of being a German.
Of being a Frenchman.
Of being an Englishman.
Of not being a German.
Of not being a Frenchman.
Of not being an Englishman.
Of being commander of the Third Company.
Of being a German mother. Of being stationed on the German Rhine. And on general principles.
Of having Otto Gebühr's* autograph.
Of having a flag. Of being a battleship. ("The proud battleship…")
Of having been an assistant quartermaster in the war.
Of being the mayor of Eggtown-on-Yolk.
Of being a member of the French Academy. (Hard to imagine.)
Of being a member of the Prussian Academy of Literature. (Unimaginable.)
Of having prevented, as a German Social Democrat, the happening of worse things.
Of being from Berne. Of being from Basel. Of being from Zurich. (And so on for all the Swiss cantons.)
Of having lost to Big Tilden.**
Of being a German. But we've already said that.

---

*   German movie actor of the 1920s and 1930s. - H.Z.
**   William Tilden (1893–1953), American tennis champion. - H.Z.

A Jew once said: "I am proud to be a Jew. If I'm not proud, I'm still a Jew—so I might as well be proud."

What reverence Frenchmen have for their language! "*Il a trouve ce mot...*" The word was there all along; the author simply found it.

In Germany, the number of war memorials is to the number of Heine memorials as force is to the spirit.

English is a simple but difficult language. It consists entirely of foreign words that are mispronounced.

A German asks: What does the man do?
An American asks: How much is he worth?
A Frenchman asks: What is his family background?
A Viennese asks: Where does he publish?
A Budapester doesn't ask; he knows the man and owes him money.

Because of inclement weather, the German revolution took place in music.

The Danes are stingier than the Italians. Spanish women indulge in illicit love more readily than German women. All Latvians are thieves. All Bulgarians stink. Rumanians are braver than Frenchmen. Russians embezzle money.
    None of this is true—but you will see it in print during the next war.

In Spain they once founded a Society for the Prevention of Cruelty to Animals. To raise the necessary funds, they arranged a big benefit bullfight.

The German thinks it up; the Italian invents it; the Englishman puts it into practice; the American buys the rights to it; the Japanese imitates it; the Spaniard won't hear of it; the Norwegian gradually gets wind of it; and the Frenchman appoints all concerned to the Académie Réaumur. Whereupon the astonished German compiles a bibliography of the whole thing.

A Norwegian in Copenhagen was shown the squat, round tower inside which one can go up in a horse-drawn carriage on a spiral ramp. "Do you have anything like this in Norway?" he was asked. "No," said the man from Oslo, piqued. "But if we did have such a tower, it would be bigger and rounder."

If American women were as good lovers as German women believe Frenchwomen to be, English women would be very pleased; they would have such a wonderful reason for feeling outraged.

The nations were invited to draw a circle.

The American appeared with a circle-drawing machine, the biggest in the world; the Englishman drew an almost perfect circle free hand; the Frenchman made a richly adorned oval; the Austrian said: "G'wan, we're not gonna bother," and traced the Englishman's circle; the Germans came up with a polygon of 1096 sides which looked like a circle but wasn't one.

Once the nations organized a competition as to who could see the farthest.

The Frenchman saw as far as the next Arrondissement. The Englishman surveyed the whole world; it reflected him. The Berliner looked from the Kurfürstendamm past the Spree as far as the Alexanderplatz and thought that in between there lay America and the Atlantic Ocean. The Viennese didn't even bother to look. He was reading about a wonderful libel suit in his newspaper.

The German destiny: to stand in front of a window in a public office. The German ideal: to sit behind such a window.

In Europe, a man is a citizen once and an alien twenty-two times. A wise man is an alien twenty-three times.

When they are buried, this is what happens:

The German has his decorations carried after him on a cushion, and even in his coffin he is proud of the funeral oration and the turnout of the mourners. The Frenchman orders a first-class funeral; the corpse notes sadly that only twenty-four candles are burning in the church. The Greek is a bit late for his funeral; he had to make a quick visit to his barber. The English lord cares about respectability and does not let on that he has died, so he remains seated dignifiedly in the House of Lords. The Viennese at first lies in his grave relatively still, but to the first worm that comes crawling along he says: "Hey you, I heard that Ada got hitched to an Italian! What? Not true, you say? Come on! To me you're just a miserable, filthy worm." Which is quite correct.

The false states of Europe: England, France, Spain, Italy, Hungary, Prussia, Estonia, Latvia, Romania, Bavaria. The boundaries are fixed. The true states of Europe: the unemployed, the workers, the employers, the profiteers on the work of others. The boundaries are fluid.

The Dutch want peace; the French want no war; the English may want no peace; and the Germans want the others to start a war against them.

A certain hotel once housed fifty members of every nationality. The English could be seen. The Germans could be heard. The French chefs could be tasted. And when there was a smell of garlic, twelve nations vied for the honor.

After the woman has surrendered, the Frenchman forgets her, the Englishman marries her, the Romanian finds her a husband, the German starts proceedings against her, and the American has married her beforehand.

When the Lord had caused the trumpet of the Last Judgment to sound, the Germans stood at attention, two abreast, with an especially nasty fellow out in front; the Englishmen came marching along in order, punctually and nonchalantly, propelling their heads in front of them with golf clubs; from the Frenchmen's corner one could hear gay hammering (they were making little holes in their third ribs in which to display their ribbons); the Swiss grumbled that they had never been wide awake before; the Spaniards just lay there, mumbling "*mofiono, mofiono*"; and the American sector of the cemetery had an illuminated sign reading:

Last Judgment Today!
Positively the Very Last in the World!
As Predicted by Pastor Higgins
of the Chicago Sunday School!
Pastor Higgins and the Good Lord Present in Person!

But when God looked upon all this, He took pity on the monkey cage and postponed the session indefinitely.

Christopher Columbus or The Discovery of America

Die Entdeckung Amerikas, 1932

A PLAY BY WALTER HASENCLEVER AND PETER PANTER

FINAL SCENE

The Golden Anchor Inn at Seville, February 5, 1505. A small, smoke-filled sailors' dive. In the background, a bar with bottles; behind it, an invisible staircase down to the cellar and to the kitchen. On the left, a large barrel from which wine is drawn. The entrance is on the right. Models of ships are suspended from the ceiling; on the walls there are pictures of seamen's life.

AMERIGO (Goes up to COLUMBUS) Permit me to introduce myself. My name is Vespucci. (Pause) Amerigo Vespucci. (Pause) I am sure you have heard of me.

COLUMBUS I'm sorry. What did you say your name was?

AMERIGO Amerigo Vespucci. The new continent was named after me. I have published a book about my expedition.

COLUMBUS Congratulations.

AMERIGO (Solemnly) Admiral, let me shake your hand. You were the first. You are truly a great man. You discovered America.

COLUMBUS I discovered what?

AMERIGO America exists. I have seen it with my own eyes.

COLUMBUS America? I discovered the sea route to Asia.

AMERIGO You discovered something far greater: a new continent.

COLUMBUS There is no new continent.

AMERIGO The calculations of the last century are in error. Asia lies somewhere else entirely.

COLUMBUS Are you trying to teach me, an old man? Here, ask my friends. Do you still remember the vow you made on our last voyage?

COOK We solemnly vowed that we reached the mainland of Asia.

DIEGO Yes, we did.

RODRIGO And we all signed it—on a big piece of parchment!

COLUMBUS (To AMERIGO) And you are trying to tell us that we weren't even in Asia! Don't be ridiculous.

AMERIGO Admiral, who are these people? They were in prison!

COLUMBUS And what about me?

AMERIGO A regrettable misunderstanding.

COLUMBUS It didn't look that way to me in prison. They treated me like the meanest criminal. They took me to Spain in chains, they deceived me and robbed me. I don't own a thing anymore. And after that I am supposed to believe it was all a mistake? No, young man. I know the score.

MARIE Admiral, would you also like some pea soup?

COLUMBUS Bring me two eggs and bread and butter.

MARIE (Calls out to PEPI) Two eggs for the admiral!

AMERIGO Why don't you write your memoirs?

COLUMBUS Memoirs? What for? I have nothing to hide.

AMERIGO So posterity might know what really happened.

COLUMBUS But things really were quite different. All the farces I've been through! No one would believe me.

AMERIGO I beg your pardon, Admiral. World history is no farce; it is something significant.

COLUMBUS What do you know about it?

AMERIGO I've written a book on the subject.

COLUMBUS And I was an eyewitness to it.

AMERIGO That isn't what matters. We need heroes to confirm our own worth. (MARIE has put two eggs, bread, and butter on the table) Besides, there are historical events that really took place. Your egg episode, for instance.

COLUMBUS What episode?

AMERIGO (Takes an egg and makes it stand on the table) Columbus's egg!

COLUMBUS What's that?

AMERIGO But Admiral, don't you remember? When mutiny broke out on the ship, someone said: "We have about as much chance of seeing land as someone has to make an egg stand on a table." Then you took an egg and put it on the table this way.

COLUMBUS Is that what I am supposed to have done? There's not a word of truth in that.

DIEGO Such fraud! Did we ever mutiny? You see what lies they tell!

CABIN BOY We were all steamed up about it.

PEPI Remember how I climbed up on the boom and yelled "Land"?

DIEGO Fellows, those were the best days of our lives!

COLUMBUS (Takes the egg, peels it, and starts eating) Mr. Amerigo, the next time you write a book, be a little more careful. That's a charming story about Columbus's egg, but unfortunately it's a fabrication from beginning to end. I'm afraid the same is true of your America.

AMERIGO I owe a profound insight to you, Admiral. One should admire great men, but never meet them. Farewell! (He goes off with a deep bow. Laughter follows him. The cabin boy picks up a guitar)

PEPI (Sings) Earth is dry and water is wet.

ALL Sante Marie!

PEPI When people come round, the stories you get!

ALL Sante Marie!

PEPI Back there, they say, there's a continent, We didn't see one, though we went. Maybe there's one just vis-a-vis...

ALL Sante Marie! Sante Marie! Lucky Sante Marie!

MARIE (Comes from behind the bar and hands COLUMBUS a book) Admiral, that must have been fascinating among the savages! Were they all naked?

COLUMBUS They weren't stark naked.

MARIE What did they have on?

COLUMBUS Swimming trunks.

MARIE (Disappointed) Oh... ! Admiral, seeing that you're such a famous man... please let me have your autograph.

COLUMBUS What do you want me to write?

MARIE It doesn't matter; I couldn't read it anyway.

COLUMBUS (Writes something in the book and hands it to her) Here, my child.

MARIE What does it say?

COLUMBUS The first one is always the fool.

MARIE Thanks a lot. (To the seamen) Well, fellows, what's to become of the country that you discovered?

DIEGO What should become of it? There's nothing but monkeys and parrots there.

PEPI Nothing can come of it. In a hundred years there won't be a soul

MARIE And what do you think, Admiral?

(COLUMBUS rises. While he speaks, a Jazz band starts playing, softly at first, then lauder and louder. The walls of the room disappear, the horizon lights up. As though by magic, a vision of New

York appears: Times Square, with skyscrapers and fiery neon advertising. It is as though the people were no longer in a tavern, but on Broadway)

COLUMBUS   Some day this land will be quiet and peaceful. I see simple, contended people. God's people living on the new soil. Here, even the poorest will be respected, and no one will go hungry or be suppressed. The people will open the gates of its treasuries and distribute gold to all countries. On the shore of its seas there will be a statue, and the words of Holy Writ will resound from its mouth: "Come to me, ye who are tired, sore, and heavy laden!" This is the world's paradise!

CURTAIN

Angler, Compleat with Piety

Der fromme Angler, 1930

There's a man near Ascona, Switzerland, who's got religion and loves all living things, all creatures great and small. Well and good. But the man happens to like fishing. So he sometimes sits by Lake Maggiore, swinging his legs, holding his fishing rod and looking into the water. And as he does so he prays.

He prays that no fish should bite.

You see, the fish are being tortured when they squirm on the hook and the man wouldn't want that. So he sends one fervent prayer after another to the Good Lord, Lake Maggiore Fish Division, to keep the fish from taking his bait. And then he goes on angling.

My dear readers! Isn't this man a typical allegory, a symbol even? That's what he is. That man must be an old Jew, or—an extreme case of Jewishness—he must have had Jesuit training. He has attained the highest level that a man can reach. He has learned how to reconcile heavenly ideals with his sinful drives, and that requires real skill. It may not make any difference to the fish wriggling on his hook, but to him it does make a difference, for now he has both: the fish and peace of mind.

Conclusion and general application: There they sit by the banks of life—or by the sea of life, that's really much better—there they sit by the sea of life, swinging their legs and dangling their lines into the water in order to hook success. But if they're shrewd, they pray at the same time, which makes them: whores who've got religion; civil-minded bank directors; democratic militarists; and journalists who oh-so-privately love truth. They prey and they pray.

Lovers in London

Liebespaar in London, 1931

I t is Saturday noon, and in Piccadilly Circus traffic is lighter; one can almost hear oneself talk, for a great centrifugal force has propelled Londoners outward: the weekend. It is the only time in the week when you can say that traffic whisks past you; nothing else is whisking here. But probably all are yearning to get out now. Goodbye, City!

Nevertheless, many are still about. The theatres on Shaftesbury Avenue offer heartrendingly beautiful plays called *Autumn Crocus* or *How Lovely Are a Bride's Tears*; these may not be the titles, but the photos displayed in the showcases look as though they were. And in front of the theatres there sit on little stools long lines of women and girls and even a few men; they are sitting in a queue because they have unreserved seats and leisure, and are waiting for the doors to open. So that they won't get bored they have brought along newspapers and cigarettes and sweets and sweethearts, and there's an old street singer who is giving them a tune; and right in the middle of the road, near the taxi stand, there is a man standing on his head—if you'll pardon the expression—and waving his legs. Hardly anyone looks at him, of course, and you mustn't think that all Londoners always stand on their heads and wave their legs; that is a mistake commonly made in travel books. This man is certainly not doing it for his health—what was it that a tap dancer said in the music hall recently? "There must be an easier way to make a living." Sure there is. So this fellow stands on his head.

And they roar past and hurry and walk and drive and run. So do I. "Excuse me!" I nearly knocked them over.

They are standing in the middle of the pavement, he and she, and all around them people flood past. They don't see them. They only have eyes for each other. I turn around slowly and stroll past them. Four times I turn around and four times I walk past them.

They don't say anything. They look at each other. All the time.

He speaks with his eyes: "Things can't go on like this," he says without opening his mouth. "It's been this way for weeks—but it can't go on like this. Something is wrong. Is there another man? Of course there is. I have an idea who it is, too. In fact, I know. Sybil! Is that what our love was meant for? Is it?" She answers with her eyes, answers little. "I don't know," she says without opening her mouth. "I don't know. I haven't anything against you." She has completely crawled into her shell, the real Sybil has withdrawn, and a token Sybil is standing there, repulsing an attack with her beautiful dark eyes. She hardly needs to repulse it—the walls are so high…

"Sybil… !" say his eyes. Hers don't say anything.

"Do you remember?" say his eyes. "Remember? Do you remember the lovely evening on the seashore when the phonograph was playing in the tent next to us and we danced to somebody else's music behind the trees? And then we danced away, farther and farther away, until the music sounded very distant through the branches. Do you remember?" Her eyes are mute. The two stand motionless in this roaring stream of humanity, and some bump into them, but they don't notice it. "Do you remember?" ask his eyes. "We walked through Hampstead. I took you home, and since that day I've known every garden fence and every post and every house on the way—and on each hangs a word from you. Do you remember?" Her eyes are lowered now, there is a veil over them; she doesn't answer. I observe him trying to make his eyes conquer—it is no use, she is the stronger one. He rears up, for he is a man—but to no avail, for she is a woman. He can't understand that. A lover can never understand that what has once been will someday be no more… after all, it used to be so. And, you fool, you think it must be forever? But nothing is forever.

They are still standing there, saying nothing and looking at each other. Luckily no one is paying attention to them—what they are doing is getting to be ridiculous. This sort of thing may be permitted on the stage—on the stage where an English audience, the most appreciative in the world, laughs when a waiter drops his tray and becomes dead serious when the violins wail and the papier-maché forest turns lilac—for that is love. On the stage, all right. But in real life? In real life one conceals one's emotions until people think one has none, for that is a sign of good breeding. And so they stand.

What is moving? The traffic that flows past the motionless couple? It's really the other way round: the traffic is motionless and they, these two, are moving. Jürgen Fehling once staged such a scene in a play by Barlach: the lovers sat at a table in the midst of a horde of carousing philistines and looked at each other. And the drinkers and toasters became quieter and quieter, finally turning into wax figures, while the lovers talked and were lively.

And in the midst of a world in busy flux, which strives for the wide open spaces there stands this group of two, stirred and with pounding hearts, in a waxen world which does not see them and which they don't see. Lost to the world, there they stand and gaze at each other; he is waiting, and she in thought is already with another with whom she hopes to become one. There they stand, ineluctably and irrevocably two, for two hearts beat as one only for seconds at a time; then the maelstrom engulfs them, the street singer croaks his song, and the heavy buses rattle and rumble past, out into the green suburbs where the English red hawthorn blooms.

Two British Bottles

Die beiden Flaschen, 1931

I n Wells…
No, not in Wales—Wales is where the well-dressed men are from. In Wells…

No, I didn't say "well"—that's what Englishmen say to start off a sentence; for in England nobody starts his sentence with the main thing. The main thing is contained in the subordinate clause. Recently I asked a young man in London whether the Number 176 bus stopped right there, at the spot where he was waiting. What do you suppose he said:

"I should hope so," he said. "Yes" would have been too definite; you can never tell, perhaps the bus won't stop. And the English language, which can be so precise, loves those dainty little back doors, although as emergency exits only—it probably makes little use of them. But then, you can always add "positively" if necessary. The other day, in a skit, someone asked: "What is the difference between a cop and a young lady? When the cop says 'stop!' he means it."

It happened in Wells, then. Wells is a sweet town in Somerset. It has a beautiful cathedral and such a peaceful air. Yet the town isn't quaint; it's almost modern and proper, everything is in good order, and it's so nice there!

So I stroll around, and instead of looking at the sights, I go window shopping—that's what I call sightseeing; you can always learn a lot that way. In the window of an antique shop was glass, and if there is glass in the window—how does the old Berlin ditty go? "If you've got an education, you'll know real good what I mean." So I buy in imagination all the glass that's there—and finally I see two dark green, jolly-looking, bulging bottles. They've got metal labels around their necks, both of them; one says "Whiskey" and the other "Gin." Gin is a distant cousin of Geneva—and as for whiskey, every man of distinction knows what that is. And because my whiskey is always housed in those tall bottles in which you buy it, I decided to acquire by purchase this green bottle, which, as you could see right off, was named Emily. Inside I went.

The English have an immortal soul and terribly irregular verbs. I spoke my piece—if my English teacher had heard it, he would have boxed my ears for sure. But the clerk understood me; he said a lot of things that I understood and some other things that I didn't—these Englishmen sometimes have such a funny accent, huh? And now the bargaining began. The bottle wasn't exactly expensive. ("How much did you pay? That interests me. You see, I gave my husband a bottle like that…" Oh, be quiet. You and your prices, all the time.) It wasn't expensive. But, but, BUT:

That whiskey bottle wasn't for sale separately; you had to buy the gin bottle with it. "Why?" I asked the man. (That was the only completely correct sentence I delivered myself of in this conversation.) Why indeed? And now the man gave me an answer so beautiful that I must record it here, an answer by which one can explain roughly half of England if one is so inclined. You would have thought he would answer: "Because I couldn't sell the other bottle by itself." Or: "Because there's more profit in it for me." Or: "These two bottles and these six glasses and that tray form a set, and I can't break it." No, nothing like that; besides, there weren't any glasses or trays. The man said: "Because they have always been together."

This answer contains everything there is about an Englishman: the unshakable firmness with which every structure remains standing until, maybe, it collapses by itself. "Because they have always been together." Because of that, these things are together even today: the Englishman and his cricket, that phenomenon of complete mystery to a foreigner, a cross between chess and a religious rite; a man and the colors of his university; a gentleman and his full dress suit when evening comes; a judge and his wig; the country and the power. "Because they have always been together."

I was deeply touched then. I thought of what might happen if I tore the bottle called Emily from the bottle named Martha; of how Martha would cry; and I couldn't answer for all that. And so I bought both bottles. "Because they have always been together."

Anyone want a gin bottle?

Part IV
Panther, Tiger & Co.

Tucholsky's desk and typewriter, at the Tucholsky Museum in Rheinsberg and a street sign and a plaque in Berlin-Mitte.

What'll I Do New Year's Eve?

Was unternehme ich Silvester?, 1921

S hall I go to the Kallmanns'? They'll light their Christmas tree, turn on the phonograph, which will scratch out "Silent Night, Holy Night." The kids will occupy the good rug with the torsos of their toys, and father will try out his new pipe. Mother Kallmann will discuss the servant problem with me, and I shall say: "Yes, ma'am... Certainly, ma'am!... Just imagine, ma'am!" All the rest she will say. No, I don't think I'll go to the Kallmanns'.

Shall I call on my girlfriend with the beautiful spirit and the fat legs? She'll have moist, big eyes and will torture me with memories. She will be in a festive mood, which doesn't really become her, and she too will light up her Christmas tree, quite ceremoniously, and say, "Dear Peter..." Boo. I don't think I'll join my beautiful spirit.

Shall I go to a public dance? There will be two thousand people crowded together in rooms designed for only two hundred. Waiters will do a brisk business selling saccharine champagne at inflated prices, and somewhere in the smoke-filled hurly-burly a band will be making noise. In the middle of the room a few people will pretend to be dancing. Everybody will be there; they will point out the VIP's from the government, film stars' names will be whispered, and the theatre will have sent its best representatives... ditto the universities... Only the call girls will behave themselves. Why talk shop on New Year's Eve if you have to do it all year round? The air will be sticky and stale, and the jokes likewise. No, I don't think I'll go to a public dance.

Shall I go to a private ball? (Oh, but I've been invited!) The rooms will have been cleared, the lamps will be draped in blue and pale violet. There will be champagne and canapés. A man at the piano, and someone playing a violin. There will be a lot of cheek-to-cheek dancing. On the rug and on the sofas, couples will be necking as though there were no beds in the whole wide world. Only those going steady will behave themselves. (People shouldn't talk.) The daughter of the house will pull out all the stops on her golden temperament; she finds it so thrilling to provide variations on the old adage "Always talk about it, but never do it." The young men will take all the liberties with the young ladies, because they don't cost anything. No, I don't think I'll go to a private ball.

Well, what then? I suggest that we fill the little blue vase with red flowers as usual and drink some quiet red wine. Perhaps you'll wake up around midnight. Then I shall say to you: "My dear, I think now I have to put on a top hat and you have to crush it for me. That's the custom." Whereupon you'll say: "I'm so tired. Good night."

And when you wake up in the morning, it will be 1922 (want to bet on it?), and I'll kiss the new year out of your eyes. And since it is an old superstition that one will be doing all year what one does on New Year's Eve, friendly and truly refreshing vistas open up to us. Happy New Year!

The Social Psychology of Holes

Zur soziologischen Psychologie der Löcher, 1931

The most important things are done through tubes. Proof: genitals, pens, and guns.
—Lichtenberg

A hole is where something isn't.
The hole is a permanent companion of the non-hole; I'm sorry, but there is no such thing as a hole by itself. If there were something everywhere, there would be no holes, but there wouldn't be any philosophy either, not to mention religion, which is holey in origin. A mouse couldn't exist without a hole, nor could man. It is the final salvation for both when they are hard-pressed by matter. A hole is always a good thing.

When a man hears the word "hole," he has associations; some think of sinkhole, others of buttonhole, still others of Goebbels.

Holes are the foundation of our social order, and that about describes some. Workers live in a hole in the wall, they always find themselves in a hole, and if they get out of line they are thrown in the hole, although they need being holed-up like a hole in the head. Being born in their slums is a curse; but why did the children have to come out of that particular hole? A few holes further on, and the kids would have been assured of going to law school.

The strangest thing about a hole is its edge. It's still part of the Something, but it constantly overlooks the Nothing—a border guard of matter. Nothingness has no such guard; while the molecules at the edge of a hole get dizzy because they are staring into a hole, the molecules of the hole get… firmy? There's no word for it.

For our language was created by the Something people; the Hole people speak a language of their own.

A hole is something static; there are no holes in transit. Well, hardly any.

Holes that got married become One—one of the strangest among the processes that cannot be imagined. If you knock down the dividing wall between two holes, does the right edge belong to the left hole? Or the left edge to the right hole? Or each to each? Or both to both? (I should have my worries!)

If a hole is plugged up, where does it go? Does it squeeze to the side and merge with matter? Or does it run to another hole to pour out its heart? What happens to the plugged-up hole? Nobody knows; there is a hole in our knowledge.

Where one thing is, there cannot be another. Where there already is one hole, can there be another?

And why are there no semi-holes?

Same objects are devalued by one little hole: because there is nothing in a single place, all the rest isn't worth anything. Examples: a railroad ticket, a virgin, a balloon.

The thing-in-itself* is still being searched for; a hole already is "in itself." Only someone with one foot in the hole and the other here among us would be truly wise; but they say that no one has managed to do this yet. Megalomaniacs claim that a hole is something negative. That is incorrect; a man is a non-hole, and the hole is the primary thing. Hole your horses! A hole is the only foretaste of paradise that we have down here. Only when you are dead will you know what living is.

Pardon this piece; I merely wanted to fill the hole between the previous selection and the next one.

---

*   Kant's concept of the "Ding an sich." –H.Z.

Psychology in the Hotel Lobby

In der Hotelhalle, 1930

W e were sitting in the lobby of the big hotel, in one of those lobbies where things always look like in the movies—the movies wouldn't have it any other way. It was twenty-five minutes past five. My companion was a neurologist; it was after his office hours, and we were drinking weak tea. It was so expensive that one could say we were having high tea. "You see," my companion was saying, "it's purely a matter of practice. They come and they go— men, women, Germans, foreigners, guests, visitors—and nobody knows them. But I know them. One glance—it's nice to have some training in psychology. I can leaf through these people as one leafs through an open book."

"And what do you read?" I asked him.

"Pretty interesting little chapters." He looked around with squinting eyes. "No riddles here—I know them all. Ask me anything."

"Well—for example: what about the man over there?"

"Which one?"

"The old man... with the whiskers—no, not that one... yes, that's the one..."

"Him?" It didn't take him a moment. "That is... as you see, the man bears a striking resemblance to old Emperor Francis Joseph. One could actually say that he is the spitting image of the Emperor... he looks... he looks like an old postman whom people consider as kind because he brings them their cheques. His bearing, his manner... I take the man to be a former court official from Vienna—a very high one, even. The collapse of the Hapsburg dynasty has affected him very, very deeply. Yes. Just look at the way he speaks with the waiter: that is an aristocrat. Unmistakably, an aristocrat. You see—in this man there is Ballhaus Square Vienna,

127

the entire culture of old Austria, the Spanish Riding School—tu, felix Austria… he is His Excellency something-or-other—some real big-shot. That's who he is."

"Amazing. Really amazing. How can you tell all that?"

He smiled, too flattered to be really flattered; how vain this man must be! "As I told you—experience, that's what it is. I acquired it in my medical practice. I'm no Sherlock Holmes, mind you. I'm just one neurologist among many, but I've got that certain look. That special eye." He smoked contentedly.

"What about the lady back there? The one sitting at the table and apparently waiting for someone—you see, she keeps looking at the door…"

"That one? My friend, you're mistaken. That lady isn't waiting for anyone—at least not here. That is, she is waiting all right, but for a miracle. Let me… just a moment…"

He pulled a monocle from his vest pocket, squeezed it on; the monocle didn't appear comfortable, and he adjusted it.

"That is… well, there is one of the few great cocottes left in the world. You know that the cocottes are dying out, like the word itself. Bourgeois competition.… Oh yes, what was I saying? A queen of love-for-sale. Less grandly put: a lady of the great, really great, demi-monde. I'll be… I'll be darned… did you see the movement of her hand? That woman devours men. Devours them. She is a… And in her eyes—just take a good look at her eyes… look at them closely… in her eyes there is a mourning complex, a whole garden full of weeping willows. This woman yearns… All those fulfillments that weren't any—that's what left her yearning. There's no doubt about that. It's problematical whether she'll ever find what she's looking for. What she wants is very hard to get—very hard indeed. This woman has had everything in life—everything. And now she wants more. That isn't easy. This muted minor mode! It could be that some man killed himself on account of her—could be—

"I can't say that exactly. I'm not omniscient; all I am is a doctor of the psyche… I should like to have loved this woman. You understand me—not to be in love with her but to have loved her. It is dangerous to love this woman. Very dangerous. Yes."

"Doctor… you are a regular Cagliostro?… your patients had better watch out."

"There's no fooling me," he said. "Not me. What else would you like to know? Now that we're in the swing…"

"The one over there! The fat man who is getting up now—he is leaving—no, he's coming back. The one with the rather ruddy face. Who do you suppose he is?"

"Well, what would you say?"

"Well… hmm… nowadays one man looks just like the next fellow… maybe…"

"Looks just like the next fellow? You just can't see—to be able to see is the whole trick. That's quite simple."

"Well then?"

"The man is a wine merchant. Either the big boss himself or the manager of a big wine firm. An energetic, well-educated man; a strong-willed man—one who seldom smiles and in spite of the wine hasn't much use for humor. A stern man. A man of the business world. Inexorable. Hates big gatherings of people. A man of seriousness. That's what he is."

"And that woman over there? The little, rather common-looking madam?"

"Panter, how can you say a thing like that? She is"—(monocle) "she's a good, decent middle-class housewife from the provinces" (monocle back to holster)—"a good woman, mother of at least four children, raised in the code of honor of petty bourgeois families—goes to church every Sunday—cooks for her husband, darns her brats' pants and dresses—everything's in good order there. That woman toes the line and keeps to the straight and narrow, she does."

"And that fellow there, doctor?"

"You see—that's the typical moneyman of our time. There you have him in the flesh. I could tell you his life story—that's how plainly I see this man's soul before me. A go-getter. One who can take hard punches. No getting him down. Doesn't waste his time with trifles; doesn't read books; doesn't give a damn about anything but his business. There you have the Americanized European. As for women—heaven's sakes! It's six o'clock. Don't be angry, but I've got an urgent appointment. Have to get a cab right away.

The check, please!" The waiter came, took the money, and left. The doctor got up.

"What do I owe you?" I asked jocularly.

"Priceless—simply priceless. Best of luck! Well, so long!" He was gone.

And then curiosity gripped me—it really did. All the analyzed victims were still there, every one of them. I sidled up to the concierge, who had a good view of the lobby from his post. And I spoke with him. And slipped something into his palm. And asked. And he answered. And I was all ears:

The Austrian courtier was a sewing machine salesman from Gleiwitz. The great whore with the mourning complex was one Mrs. Bimstein from Chicago; now her husband had joined her at her table—unmistakably Mr. Bimstein. The manager of the big wine firm was Grock, the clown. The cushiony mama was the proprietress of a hospitable etablissement in Marseille. The go-getting financier was a poet of the avant-garde.

And only the psychologist was a psychologist.

What Do Women Do Before Going Out?

Was tun Frauen, bevor sie ausgehen?, 1924

When a woman has known for four hours that she and her husband are leaving for the theatre at seven o'clock, and when her exhausted husband comes rushing home from the office at six-thirty to pick her up, what does such a woman do?

She displays limitless activity.

First she starts to make up. The concept of make-up includes a series of inexplicable processes and activities which can never be completely fathomed—to wit: plucking the hair before a large mirror, ditto before a small one; picking up a random object and putting same down; searching for the keys; rummaging through a chest; trying on and rejecting a hat before the large mirror; busily running through all rooms. And this is where the puzzle, the great, unfathomable puzzle, begins: Why do women do things at the last moment which they could have done an hour before and which take up far more time than is possibly available? Why?

6:45 p.m.: "I've got to clean my gloves with benzene. Anna! Anna! Where's the benzene?" The benzene bottle, the gloves, and a large, ugly, evil looking rag. Sure enough: it makes vicious benzene smudges and refuses to do what is asked of it. This takes ten minutes.

6:55 p.m.: "I think I'd better wear the new gloves after all." In the background an unfortunate man wrings his hands—why wasn't this done ten minutes ago... ? A reproachful look: "You simply don't understand!" No, he simply doesn't.

7:08 p.m: "The laundry hasn't been sorted yet!" My dear child... Never mind, "dear" and never mind "child"—the laundry hasn't been sorted yet! Does this have to be done now? It's now or never. "Anna! Five panties, forty-four towels—how come forty-four? Oh, yes—twenty-three handkerchiefs, five children's shirts—well, I'll do that tomorrow, put them down here for now! Anna, have we settled accounts? Well, tomorrow we'll have the brisket of beef that's left over..." In the background: God Almighty, what have I done to deserve this? Why have you punished me, my good Lord? My dear child, it is now twenty past seven... "Then you should have come home from the office earlier!"

And there's nothing that can be done about it.

Dear Herr Panter:

I read your little newspaper piece entitled "What Do Women Do Before Going Out?" I must tell you that you certainly don't seem to know every woman. Today, thank goodness, there are a lot of women and girls who are at least as punctual and reliable as men are. The large number of female employees of the telephone company are proof of this.

Unfortunately I must end my letter. My husband has just arrived and tells me that it is time to go to our Wednesday Club. If that had not interfered, Herr Panter, I would have written you quite differently and in far greater detail, but unfortunately I must close now and go with my husband. I should merely like to tell you that as far as organization and punctuality are concerned, the great majority of women are a match for any man a hundred times over. I for one am always there on the dot and never start picking up and then putting down a thousand things just before leaving. Actually, making fun of women all the time is male presumptuousness. Why don't you men start looking among yourselves; you'll certainly find plenty of vices and faults! And another thing, Herr Panter: a woman who runs a household simply has a lot burdens and worries which no one relieves her of, not even her own husband. She has to do almost everything herself, and therefore it might occasionally happen that she is late for some amusement. And what harm is done if once in a while her husband has to wait a bit for her? Surely a man can be that chivalrous toward his wife, especially if she slaved all day to make a home for him. For the rest, women are much more punctual than you men are!

That's that. Now I shall quickly get this letter ready for mailing, for I still have to get dressed and do my hair.

A Punctual Woman

Apprehension

Befürchtung, 1929

S hall I know how to die? Sometimes I fear that I shan't. This is what I ask myself at such times: how will you act? Oh, I don't mean your boring life… something-or-other while you yourself die—not the minute before a gas attack, with your pants full of courage and your heroically distorted face turned toward the foe—not that way. No, merely that senseless process in bed: fatigue, pain, and now that thing. Will you know how to do it?

As an example: for years I wasn't able to sneeze properly. I sneezed like a small dog with the hiccups. And—if you'll pardon the expression—until my twenty-eighth year I didn't know how to belch; then I met Charlie, an old fraternity man, and he taught me. But who is going to teach me how to die?

Oh yes, I've seen it done. I've been to an execution, and I have seen sick people die—it seemed as if they had a very hard time of it. But what will happen if I behave so clumsily that nothing comes of it? After all, that's conceivable.

"Don't worry, my good man. It will sink down upon you, this hard thing. You have a false conception of death. It will…" Is somebody speaking from experience here? It is the truest of all democracies, this democracy of death. That accounts for the vast superiority of the priests who act as if they had died a hundred times already, as if they had their information from the beyond—and now they play the messengers of death among the living.

Perhaps it won't be so hard, after all. A doctor will help me die. And if my pain is not too great, I shall wear an embarrassed and modest smile and say: "Please excuse me—it is my first time…"

There is No Virgin Snow

Es gibt keinen Neuschnee, 1931

If you climb upward and look around, breathing deeply and thinking what a fine fellow you are to have scaled such heights, you alone—then you always discover footprints in the snow. Someone has been there before you.

Have faith in God. Despair of Him. Reject all philosophy. Let the doctor tell you that you have stomach cancer and that it will be all over in four years. Believe in a woman. Despair of her. Carry on with two women. Plunge into the world. Withdraw from it…

All these experiences someone has had before you; this is the way someone believed, doubted, laughed, cried, and pensively picked his nose—just the same way. Someone has always been there.

That makes no difference, I know. You're experiencing it for the first time. For you it is virgin snow that lies there. But it really isn't, and this discovery is very painful at first.

There once was a poor Jew in Poland who had no money to go to school, but his mind was burning with mathematics. He read the few meager books that he was able to get, and he studied and meditated on his own. And one day he invented something, he discovered an entirely new system, and he felt: there I've found something. And when he left his little town and got out into the world, he saw new books, and what he had discovered by himself already existed: it happened to be differential calculus. And he died—of consumption, people said. But that wasn't the cause.

It is at its most peculiar in solitude. You're quite ready to acknowledge that people have their standard experiences in the hustle and bustle of life. But if one is as alone as you are, if one meditates like this, taking death into account, withdrawing this way, trying to look up ahead—then, one would think he had reached altitudes on which the foot of man has never trod. But there are always foot-prints, someone has always been there, someone has always climbed higher than you have been able to, much higher.

That mustn't discourage you. Climb, scale, keep on climbing. But there is no top. And there is no virgin snow.

The Fifth Season

Die fünfte Jahreszeit, 1929

The most beautiful time of life, of the year? Let me search my feelings. Spring? That tall, somewhat anaemic lummox? He stalks over the green hills with a wreath of paper blossoms on his head, with a yellow stick in his hand—pre-Raphaelite and like an escapee from the Welfare Department; everything is light blue and loud, the sparrows chirp and wallow in blue puddles, buds burst open with a little pop, little green leaves saucily stick their little heads out... aw, phooey! The earth looks as though it needed a shave, the rain it raineth every day and acts as though the earth owed it a living: "I'm so necessary for growth." Spring?

Summer? The land lies there like a cow with calf; the fields are busy and so are the larvae and the starlings. The way that the scarecrows scare crows makes the older birds split their sides laughing. The oxen are sweating, the steam ploughs go "Moa," great activity has set in all around. At night, when the fog lifts, there is still a rumbling in the belly of the earth; the whole land steams with labor, it grows, copulates, bears young; ferments rise and fall, mares brood, cows sit on their eggs, ducks give birth to live litter—little quacking balls of wool. The rooster—the rascal, he is really the symbol of summer, he has the elixir of the gods to offer; he is the symbol of fertility, he'll have you know, and accordingly makes a hell of a racket. Summer?

Autumn? Peevishly, the folds of the land contract; the chilly earth wraps itself in thin veils; showers sweep over the fields and lash the denuded trees which raise their wooden fingers in an oath of manifestation: no resources here. And that's the way it looks: no resources. And the wind sues the earth; plaintively he roars around corners; he burrows into narrow nasal passages and goes "Grrr" in sinuses, for he gets a commission from nose-and-throat specialists. Brown street muck spurts up high... The sun is taking the sun on the Riviera. Autumn?

And Winter? It supplies a kind of snow which, on seeing the earth at a distance, immediately dissolves into slush; when it gets cold, it isn't good and cold, but wet and cold—wet, really... If you step on the ice, it goes "crack" and develops holes and cracks—that's the quality you get. Sometimes there is glare ice; then the Good Lord, the dear old man, sits in the cotton-candy clouds and enjoys watching people fall on their faces. The east wind is cold, so are the sun's rays, but the central heating is the coldest of all. Winter?

"In a word, Herr Hauser? Here you have our four seasons. If you please: which one?"

"None of these. The fifth."

"There's no such thing."

"Oh, but there is a fifth season. Listen."

When Summer is past and the harvest has been garnered, when nature lies down like an old, tired workhorse in the stable, when Indian Summer is dying away and early Autumn hasn't set in yet— then it is the fifth season.

It is a time of rest. Nature holds her breath; on other days it breathes imperceptibly with a gently heaving breast. Now all is over: the giving birth, the maturing, the growing, the spawning, the harvesting—now it is done. The leaves and the grasses and the shrubs are still there, but at the moment they are not fulfilling a function. Whether or not there is any higher purpose in nature—at the moment the wheels are not turning. They are standing still.

Gnats play in the black-golden light; in the light there really are black tones: deep old gold lies under the beech trees, plum-blue on top of the hills. Not a leaf is stirring, it is quite still. The colors are shining, the lake is as though painted, it is quite still. A boat is gliding downstream; what has been stored up is being expended; it is a time of rest.

This goes on for four, maybe eight, days.

And then something happens.

One morning you can smell autumn in the air. It isn't cold yet; it isn't windy; nothing has changed, really, and yet everything is different. It seems as if something in the air has snapped—something has happened. The die kept its balance that long, it tottered... there... there... and now it has fallen on to the other side. Everything still seems as it was yesterday: leaves, trees, shrubs... but now everything is different. The light is bright; gossamer threads float through the air. Everything has given a jerk; the magic is gone, the spell is broken; now it passes into clear autumn. How many will be granted you? This is one of them. The miracle lasted four days, maybe five, and you were wishing that it might never, never cease. It is the time of year when ageing gentlemen wax quite sentimental, but it isn't late love, it is something else. Call it optimistic intimation of death, a joyous recognition of the end. Indian summer, early autumn, and what lies in between. A very short time span in the year. It is the fifth and most beautiful season.

Husband and Wife Tell a Joke

Ein Ehepaar erzählt einen Witz, 1931

Herr Panter, we heard such a cute joke yesterday, we've simply got to tell it to you—I've got to tell it. My husband knew it already—but it's just too cute. Listen now. A man—Walter, don't drop tobacco on the rug—you're dropping tobacco on the rug—well, a man—no, a mountain climber—loses his way in the mountains. He's in the mountains and gets lost, in the Alps. What's that? In the Dolomites, not in the Alps?—what's the difference? So he walks through the darkness, and he sees a light and goes right up to it—let me tell it! That's part of it!—he goes up to it, and he sees a hut in which peasants live, a farmer and his wife. The farmer is old and she is young and pretty—yes, she's young. They're already in bed. No, they're not in bed…"

"My wife can't tell jokes. Let me tell it. Afterwards you can say if I told it right. So I'm going to tell it to you. Well, a man wanders around in the Dolomites and loses his way. So he comes—you got me all mixed up, it doesn't go like that at all! The joke's quite different. In the Dolomites—that's the way it goes!—in the Dolomites there lives an old farmer with his young wife. And they haven't got anything to eat; they've only a can of beef to last them till the next market day. And they're saving that. And there comes—what do you mean? I'm telling it right! Keep quiet. And there comes a wanderer at night—there's a knock at the door, it's a man who's lost his way, and he asks to be put up for the night. But they've got no room, that is, they have only one bed in which the two of them are sleeping. What? Trudy, but that's nonsense! It can be very nice!"

"Well, I couldn't. Always to have someone there who… kicks in his sleep—well, I just couldn't."

"Nobody's asking you to. Don't interrupt me all the time."

"But you said it could be nice. I don't think so."

"Well…"

"Walter, the ashes! Why can't you get an ashtray?"

"Well, the wanderer is standing in the hut, he is dripping from the rain, and he'd like to spend the night there. And the farmer tells him he could sleep in the bed, with his wife."

"No, that's not the way it was, Walter, you're telling it wrong! In the middle, between him and his wife—the wanderer was supposed to sleep in the middle!"

"All right, in the middle, for all I care. What's the difference?"

"There is a difference—the whole joke's based on it."

"But the joke isn't based on where the man sleeps."

"Of course it is! How is Herr Panter supposed to understand the joke… let me—I'll tell it. So the man, you understand, sleeps between the old farmer and his wife. And outside there's a thunderstorm. Let me continue!"

"She's telling it quite wrong. First there's no storm, but they fall asleep quietly. Suddenly the farmer wakes up and says to his wife—Trudy, answer the telephone, it's ringing—No, of course he doesn't say that… The farmer says to his wife—Who is it? Who's calling? Tell him to call back—we're busy now. Yes. No. Yes. Hang up. Why don't you hang up?"

"Has he finished telling you the joke? He hasn't? Well, go ahead!"

"So the farmer says: 'I've got to go out to look after the goats—I think they've broken loose and then we'll be without milk tomorrow. I'll see if the stable door is locked right.'"

"Walter, excuse me for interrupting, but Paul says he can't call back later, he can't call before tonight."

"All right, tonight, then. So the farmer—please have some more coffee! So the farmer goes out, and no sooner has he gone than the young wife nudges…"

"Wrong. Dead wrong. She doesn't, the first time. He goes out, but she doesn't nudge him until the third time—you see, the farmer goes out three times—that's what I thought such a big laugh! Let me! So the farmer goes out, to look after the goat; and the goat is there; and he comes in again."

"No, he doesn't; he stays out a long time. Meanwhile, the young wife says to the wanderer..."

"She doesn't say anything. The husband comes in.. ."

"At first he doesn't come in!"

"Well, the farmer comes in, and after sleeping awhile, he suddenly gives a start and says: 'I've got to look after the goat again'—and out he goes."

"You completely forgot to tell that the wanderer is awfully hungry!"

"Yes. The wanderer said before supper he was so awfully hungry, and they told him there was a little cheese left."

"And milk."

"And milk, and some canned meat, too, but he couldn't have that because it would have to last them till the next market day. And then they went to bed."

"And when the farmer was outside, she gives him, that is, the wanderer, a nudge and says: 'Well...'"

"You're way off. Way off. Walter, that's quite wrong. She doesn't say: 'Well...'"

"Of course she says 'Well...' What else would she say?"

"She says: 'Now this would be an opportunity.'"

"On the contrary. She says: 'Well...' and gives the wanderer a nudge."

"You really spoil every joke, don't you, Walter?"

"I beg our pardon? I spoil every joke?! You're the one who spoils them—not me! So the woman says..."

"Now let me tell that joke. You're botching up the punch line."

"Now don't get me mad, Trudy! If I start telling a joke, I want to finish it, too!"

"But you weren't the one who started it—I did!"

"It doesn't matter—in any case, I want to finish the story, because you can't tell jokes, not properly, anyway!"

"So I tell stories in my own way and not in yours, and if you don't like it, you don't have to listen!"

"I don't want to listen—I want to finish telling the story—and so that Herr Panter will enjoy it."

"If you think it's any fun listening to you..."

"Trudy!"

"Now I'm asking you, Herr Panter, is that bearable? He's been so jumpy all week, I have…"

"You are…"

"Your lack of control…"

"In a second she's going to say: Complexes! Bad upbringing, that's what your mother calls it…"

"My upbringing… !"

"Who was it that stopped the legal proceedings? Who did? Was it me? No, it was you! You were the one who asked that the divorce…"

"That's a lie!"

Wham!—the door flies shut on the right. Bang!—goes the door on the left. Here I sit, with half a joke. Wonder what the man said to the young farmer's wife?

Essay on Man

Der Mensch, 1931

Man has two legs and two sets of convictions: one for good times and one for bad ones. The latter is called Religion.

Man is a vertebrate animal and has an immortal soul, as well as a fatherland, just so he won't get too cocky.

Man is produced in a natural way, but he considers it unnatural and doesn't like to talk about it. He is made, but he isn't asked whether he wants to be.

Man is a useful creature, because he serves to make oil stocks rise through war casualties, to increase mine owners' profits through mining casualties, as well as serving culture, art, and science.

Besides the urges to procreate and to eat and drink, man has two passions: to make noise and to not listen. One could just about define man as a creature that never listens. A wise man does well not to listen, because he seldom gets to hear anything sensible. What men like to hear are promises, flattery, appreciation, and compliments. When flattering, it is advisable that one pile it on three grades thicker than one would think it be utmost possible.

Man begrudges his kind everything, which is why he invented laws. He mustn't, so the others shouldn't either.

To rely on man, one does well to sit on him; then one is certain, at least for a little while, that he won't run away. Some also rely on his character.

Man breaks down into two parts: a male part, which doesn't want to think, and a female one which is unable to. Both have so-called emotions; the surest way to arouse them is to sensitize certain nerve spots of the organism. In such cases, some men secrete lyric poetry.

Man is a herbivorous and carnivorous creature. On North Pole expeditions he occasionally devours specimens of his own kind; but this is compensated for by Fascism.

Man is a political animal, which likes best to spend its life massed into clumps. Each clump hates the other clumps because they are the others, and hates its own clump because it is its own. This latter hatred is called Patriotism.

Every man has a liver, a spleen, a pair of lungs, and a flag; all four organs are vital. There are said to be men without a liver or a spleen and with only one lung; there are no men without a flag.

Man likes to stimulate weak procreative activity, and for this he has various resources: bullfights, crime, sports, and jurisprudence.

Men conjointly do not exist. There are only men who master and others who are mastered. But no one has yet mastered himself, because the opposing slave is always mightier than the domineering master. Every man is his own inferior.

When man feels that he can no longer kick up his heels, he becomes pious and wise; then he gives up the sour grapes of the world. This is called contemplation. Man's various stages of life regard one another as different races; oldsters usually have forgotten that they were young once, or they forget that they are old, and young people never comprehend that they can grow old.

Man doesn't like to die because he doesn't know what happens afterward. If he imagines he does, he still doesn't like to die, because he wants to continue for a little while longer in the old way. For "a little while longer," read "forever."

For the rest, man is a creature that knocks, makes bad music, and lets his dog bark. Sometimes he leaves you in peace, but then he is dead. Besides men there are Saxons and Americans, but we won't take them up until next year when we have Zoology.

Bread and Tears

Brot mit Tränen, 1926

Sometimes, when something terrible has happened, one has to eat afterwards. It is a strange way of eating…

Disgust with everyday living, shame at being subjected to it—these have been overcome; for at first it hurt so, this thought of eating something now, after such a happening. Then the vessel of pain fulfills a formality.

It can't be called eating. Certainly your body is supplied with nourishment, that's true, and it even goes down. But your tear-veiled eyes are still burning, salty drops fall on your sandwich, it is only the length of your nose from pathos to trivia. Your cheeks are chewing, your throat is swallowing, your hand is grasping something bread-like. But it doesn't taste like anything; it is a useless gesture, this eating. It disgusts you, this thing.

Once a relative of mine lost her husband. It happened at seven o'clock. When he was dead, they all sat down at the table, out of necessity, as after a battle fought and lost. It was all over. No one said a word. But then someone spoke, and I'll never forget the voice of the woman who said, sobbed, tearfully moaned to her sister: "Where did you get these eggs?" "At Prusterman's. Is there something wrong with them?" See, this is the way life fetches back its people who go an vacation to the land of mourning.

The Most Famous Man in the World

Der berühmteste Mann der Welt, 1922

The most famous man in the world is not a parliamentarian or a politician, neither Wilson nor Poincare, not an inventor, a tenor, or an airplane pilot. The most famous man undoubtedly is Mr. Charlie Chaplin, a man everybody has laughed about at some time or other: Parisians and Londoners, all Americans and Australian sailors, Chinese moviegoers, and in recent years the Germans as well—the old continent and the new. And that Mars has not laughed at him yet is due only to faulty communication with that movieless piece of real estate.

This is what Mr. Chaplin is like:

A smallish man with a little black hat, a little cane, and a little moustache appears on the scene. He walks as no one has ever walked before on this earth: he waddles quickly and hastily and two feet whose tips are turned completely outward. He has dark, almost sad eyes, and he faces the world worriedly, because trouble is just around the corner. Yes, there it is.

Trouble is a fat man, a coarse fellow of enormous dimensions with whom Mr. Chaplin immediately comes to blows. The reason is not quite clear; nothing is quite clear in these pictures. But what matters is not their lack of plot, the tangle of thrashings, fire hoses, young girls, spilling milk bottles, and falling plaster busts. What matters is he, Mr. Chaplin.

From the eight or ten films that have been shown in Germany thus far, one remembers a wealth of details; each of which is acted to perfection.

Mr. Chaplin loads thirteen chairs on his back, looks like a chaircupine a la Christian Morgenstern, and bristles with chair-leg quills. Mr. Chaplin has escaped from an American jail where the prisoners have to wear striped clothing, and the next morning he wakes up in bed; depressed and astonished, his dark, intelligent eyes move over his striped pajamas and the latticed bars of his bed. It's true, then? Back in prison? But no; a servant brings him coffee, And the way Mr. Chaplin immediately turns from a cowering fugitive into a fine gentleman, with one shrug of his shoulders, an all but imperceptible pulling together in his eyes—that is simply masterful.

A hungry Mr. Chaplin has to watch a fat man eat a twenty-four-course breakfast; then he is supposed to clear away the empty dishes. One look, two spoons, and with a victorious mien Mr. Chaplin begins to play xylophone on the plates.

All these ideas take only an instant; everything goes by quite swiftly and is executed with the greatest economy of means. He has barricaded himself behind an overturned kitchen table and pelts his partners with fried potato dumplings. Suddenly the association "trench" flashes up within him. He picks up two empty wine bottles, raises his head over the table, and with consummate strategy spies on the enemy through this novel periscope, whereupon he dives down again quick as lightning.

He has developed a comedy of inactivity that is simply tremendous. The man who is afraid to go through a door, who starts out three times and turns back four, has never been played the way Chaplin portrays him. He is sitting at the Salvation Army and has to laugh at something that is happening next to him; the reproachful eyes of the preacher are on him. Close-up: you see his cheerful grin, and then the laughter seems to have been snipped off by a pair of pliers. A reprimanded schoolboy shifts about in his seat uneasily—and whole nations roll in the aisles.

It is utterly incomprehensible how he achieves these effects. Sometimes it is only a small movement; he can cry with his shoulders. Once he is about to get a massage; Chaplin sees the giant masseur and his slapped, manhandled victim. It's his turn next... And in his unfathomable eyes there is such fear, such a deep, almost animal fear, along with a pinch of irony at the fact that such a thing can be... He does not stir, and one can hear him think his every thought.

He is so kind and friendly to everybody! Next to him there is a little dog made of cloth, a children's toy. There also is a leaky bottle that soils his pants. Shocked and angry he looks at the dog. Then it turns out that it was the bottle after all. And with an infinitely tender, gentle stroking movement he begs the little dog's pardon…

That man must have a tremendous gift of observation, purloining eyes. He can imitate the motions of all occupations. At one time he combs the hair of a bearskin rug by the bedside: with what feminine grace and blasé matter-of-factness he handles the comb and the brush, and after shampooing dries the wet hair with light, deft, elegant touches! That displays the natural comic instinct of this great artist. When our mimes imitate a craftsman on the stage, it is evident that they have never watched one; no shoemaker hammers that way, no scribe writes like that, these are not the movements of a coachman. Chaplin knows them all.

He manages to render other people ridiculous by his very appearance. He merely appears with his little hat, his little cane, his little moustache; he waddles on his preposterous legs—and suddenly everyone around him is in the wrong and he is in the right; the whole world has become ludicrous. There is a wartime drawing of him on which the artist has depicted the German Kaiser and his generals, with bristling moustaches and awe-inspiring helmets. Their eyes almost pop out of their heads as they all look at one thing. In front of them Chaplin is shuffling through the room, softly whistling to himself and swinging his cane with indescribable insolence. And all militarism has gone plop.

"All the nonsense which Mr. Chaplin creates derives from his unsuccessful attempts to be just like other people" (St. John Ervine). He once saw how a bartender mixes drinks and how in the mad whirl of ice cubes, cherry punch, silver cups, and sleight of hand he briefly smells each egg before throwing it in the bucket… Aha, this is how it's done. And when he, Chaplin, mixes drinks, he too smells the egg—but before he cracks it. Doesn't really matter, in the heat of battle…

They say that he gives all his movies a trial run before children. If that is not true, it is a brilliant fabrication. For these films, with their pensive comedy, their funny tragedy, address themselves to the child in every man, to that which has presumably remained the same among all peoples: the indestructible vigor of youth. Chaplin presents the most primitive things, but he does so with genius. And he shows how ridiculous it is to be an adult who takes himself seriously.

Once, when he was returning to Los Angeles from Europe, two hundred small boys greeted him at a small American station, all of them disguised as Mr. Chaplin: a little hat, a little moustache, and a little cane. This is how they waddled up to him. And because he really loves children, he said "Hello" to all of them.

Like all great comedians, he is a philosopher. Don't miss seeing him. You will laugh yourself sick and will be grateful to him for this laughter as long as you live.

There he goes after all the trouble, tugging at his little hat, waddling off, his legs saying "Goodbye!"

How To Make a Bad Speech

Ratschläge für einen schlechten Redner, 1930

N ever begin at the beginning, but always three miles before it. Something like this:

"Ladies and gentlemen! Before I come to my subject for tonight let me speak briefly…"

Here you have just about everything that makes for a nice beginning: the announcement that you intend to speak and what you intend to say; and the little word "briefly." That way you instantly win the hearts and ears of your audience.

For this is what your listeners like: to be given your talk like a hard assignment in school, to be threatened with what you are going to say, are saying, and have said already. Always make things as complicated as you can.

Don't speak without notes—that disturbs people. The best thing is to read off your speech. That is safe and reliable; then, too, everybody is happy if the reading speaker looks up suspiciously after every half sentence to make sure everyone is still there.

If you absolutely won't take this friendly advice and simply, positively must speak without notes (You amateur! You silly Cicero! Why don't you follow the example of our professional speakers, the Reichstag delegates; have you ever heard any of them make an impromptu speech? Why, they probably write down their cries of "Hear! Hear!" in advance)—anyway, if you must speak freely, then speak the way you write. And I know just how you write.

Speak in long, involved sentences—sentences of which you, who have prepared them at home, enjoying the leisure which you need so much, and not paying any attention to the children, know the end very well, but the construction of which your listeners, impatiently daydreaming in their seats and feeling transported back to college classes in which they once liked to doze, find baffling. Well, this is just a fair sample of how you've got to speak.

Always start with the ancient Romans and, no matter what you are talking about, supply the historical background. That is not merely the German way, but that of all bespectacled creatures. Once I listened to a Chinese student give a lecture at the Sorbonne; he spoke good, fluent French, but to everyone's joy he began like this: "Let me give you a very brief account of the history of my Chinese homeland since the year 20,000 BC." He looked up in surprise, because people were laughing so hard.

You, too, must do it that way. Right you are: otherwise they won't know what you are talking about. Who on earth can understand all that without the historical background? Of course! People didn't come to your lecture for a slice of life, but to hear what they can look up in books—quite right. Always give 'em history, give it to 'em.

Never worry about whether the current that runs from you to the audience comes back to you—that's a piddling detail. Speak without regard for the effect you have, for the people, for the air in the hall. Speak away, my good man. You'll get your reward in heaven.

You must put everything into secondary clauses. Never say: "Taxes are too high." That would be too simple. Say: "I'd like to add to what I've just said that taxes seem to be far too…" That's the way.

From time to time show people how to drink a glass of water. That is something they like to see.

If you should make a joke, be sure to laugh in advance, so that people will be sure to recognize the punch line.

A speech is a monologue—how could it be otherwise? After all, only one person is talking. Even after fourteen years of speaking in public you couldn't be expected to know that a speech is not only a dialogue, but an orchestral composition; you see, a silent mass joins in all the time. And you've got to hear that. But no, you needn't. Speak away, read away, keep thundering, keep historicizing.

To what I have just said about the technique of public speaking I should like to add briefly that a lot of statistics can't help but add class to a speech. It is most reassuring, and since everyone is quite capable of retaining ten different statistics without effort, it is quite a lot of fun.

Announce the finish of your speech well ahead of time, so your listeners won't burst a blood vessel out of sudden joy. (Paul Lindau once started one of those notorious wedding toasts with the words "And in conclusion..."). Announce the conclusion, then start all over again and speak for another half hour. This can be repeated several times.

Don't just make an outline of your speech; let your audience in on it, too. That adds flavor.

Never speak for less than an hour and a half, otherwise it would hardly be worth bothering to start.

While one is speaking, the others have to listen. That is your golden opportunity. Misuse it!

HOW TO MAKE A GOOD SPEECH

Main clauses. Main clauses. Main clauses.

A clear outline in your head—as little as possible on paper.

Facts, or an appeal to the emotions. A slingshot or a harp. A speaker shouldn't be an encyclopaedia. People have one at home.

Listening to one voice is fatiguing; never speak for more than forty minutes. Don't strive for any effects that aren't part of your makeup. The speaker's platform is a merciless thing; a man is more naked on it than in a solarium.

Remember Otto Brahm's motto: "What's been cut can't flop."

The Briefcase

Die Aktenmappe, 1932

This is what happened this afternoon. I went to my dentist's office—an hour's ride on a commuter train. The man gave me novocaine, drilled, hammered, and pulled—all very nice. Then we parted as good friends and, despite everything, I went to have some lunch. Because he had told me not to, I drank two little snifters of schnapps. (Certainly the wrong thing to do.) Then I boarded the train. Tired isn't the word for it. I tried to read a very refined society novel set in hotels that would never admit me. Whether it was that, the two glasses of schnapps, or the novocaine—anyway, I was soon sound asleep and didn't wake up until the accustomed rattling had stopped. I looked at the name of the station… My God! Coat, hat, out… just in time; the train wasn't moving yet. Then I took a look at myself and got a strange feeling… That wasn't my overcoat. It was lilac-colored and mine isn't. How embarrassing! My mind worked like a flash: the train is about to leave; you'll go to the stationmaster and explain the situation to him; he'll telephone ahead to the last stop and the coats will be exchanged. Surely that can… The train hadn't left yet, and so I jog-trotted back and muttered in embarrassment, "I've… excuse me," took off and put on. The real owner of the purloined overcoat must have been snoozing in a corner, for the other gentleman only grinned apathetically. Out. The train wasn't moving yet. And then I took a look at myself and found that I had a brown briefcase in my hand. And it wasn't mine, for I didn't have a briefcase.

I returned it, of course, for there still was time. But one question arises: suppose no one at the police station had known me. And suppose I was out of work. And suppose this is a true story: who would believe that sort of thing?

Oh yes, tired... And right after lunch. And the novocaine. Sure. The prosecutor: "Did you have a briefcase when you went to see the dentist?"

I'll have to answer no. The judge: "Do you usually travel with a briefcase?" I have to reply in the negative. Well, all this is hypothetical. There would never have been a trial, for I would immediately have turned the briefcase in to the stationmaster. I am simply supposing this, that, and the other thing, and here are my conclusions: every day we do many unreasonable things. We don't pay attention. Each of us does things that don't make the slightest sense. (That we make up for them later is another matter.) However, in a court, trial witnesses and defendants should never be exempted from that rule. And if a defendant or a witness says things that at first seem utterly idiotic ("Surely you're not trying to tell us..."), these should first be examined. There are, of course, outright lies. But as regards symptomatic acts (called Freudian slips), particularly false observations... that is a grey area. Be careful, judges! Be careful, public opinion! Let us be careful, all of us! For years I walked by a door in our house without noticing it. One day I did notice it. If I had been called as a witness before that day and asked "Is there a door down there, in such and such a place?", I would have testified under oath: "No, there's no door there." Doesn't everyone have that kind of experience at one time or another? Everyone does. It can happen to anyone.

On my way home I was very ashamed of myself and reflected that this is why one ought to think before telling anyone, "You're lying! That's impossible! You walked by that door for years and are trying to tell us that you didn't see it? That's why one ought to give a lot of careful thought before telling anyone, "You were on the train and took along a handbag that doesn't belong to you, and then you're trying to tell us that it was an accident? Such an oversight never happened to me!" One happened to me today.

Memo to Juries

Merkblatt für Geschworene, 1929

Other papers please copy

I f you should be a juryman, don't believe that you are God. That you are sitting next to the judge and that the defendant is in front of you is pure chance—it could just as well be the other way round.

If you are a juror, remember that any man, yourself included, is captivated by externals. A defendant with flaming red hair who drools when he speaks is not a prepossessing person; don't make him pay for that.

If you serve on a jury, always remember that the defendant over there is not the first and only one of his kind; such cases confront juries every single day; so don't be thunderstruck because someone has committed a shameful act, even though you yourself may never have come in contact with such a thing.

Every crime has two bases: the biological inheritance of a man and the social milieu in which he lives. Where moral guilt comes in, you can hardly ever judge—none of us can, unless he happens to be an experienced psychoanalyst or a very wise father-confessor. You are only a juror; don't punish, but do protect society from lawbreakers.

Before you act as a juryman, try in every way you can to inspect a jail or a house of correction; permission isn't easy to obtain, but it can be done. Be sure you know exactly what the punishment that you mete out is like; read some autobiographies of jail inmates. Only then can you give your verdict.

If you serve on a jury, don't let the philosophy of your class and your associations stand as the only possible one. There are others—some may be worse, others better, but in any case, they are different.

Don't believe in the deterrent effect of your verdict; there isn't any. Never yet has an evil-doer let any threatened punishment keep him from pulling something off. Don't you believe that you or the judges are charged with the task of avenging a crime—leave this to the celestial powers. The only blessed thing you have to do is to protect society. The seclusion of the evil-doer from society is temporary protection.

If you are a juror, inform yourself before the court session about the rights that you have—interrogation of witnesses and so forth.

The hearing of evidence often lays bare the private lives of strangers before you. Remember: if they were to spread your own letters, your conversations, your little love affairs and marital troubles in front of strangers, they would look very, very different from what they really are. Don't be quick to take every word seriously—all of us say more than we could answer for under oath. Don't look on every woman who has been tipsy once as a whore; don't see a burglar in every unemployed man; don't see a swindler in every overly shrewd businessman. Think of yourself.

If you are a juror, see two things in the judge: a man who has more experience in juridical logic than you have, and a man who may err because he is in a rut. The judge knows the ins and outs of crime better than you do—that is his advantage; he has become blunted and is usually confined by the narrow views of his little castle of officialdom—that is his disadvantage. You are there to make up for this.

Don't stand in awe of the judge. You have exactly the same rights on this day. He is not your superior; take away his robe and his round cap and he is a human being like you. Don't let him treat you like a fool. Express your opinion even if the judge cites legal paragraphs and decisions of the federal courts to prove that you are wrong—federal court decisions aren't much good, anyway. You are not obliged to govern yourself according to them. Try to bring your colleagues round to your way of thinking—you have that right. Speak clearly and to the point, and say whatever you wish—don't bore the jury and the judges with long speeches during your deliberations.

You are to give a judgment only of the defendant's deed, not of his behavior in court. Sentence may be pronounced only on the basis of a paragraph in the penal code; in Germany, there is no crime labeled "Insolent behavior in court." The defendant has the following rights which judges like to deprive him of, usually for reasons of convenience: he may deny charges; he may refuse to answer; he may be "stubborn." A confession is never grounds for a lighter sentence; this is something the judges have invented to save themselves work. Nor is a confession a sign of repentance; from the outside one can hardly tell when a man is repentant, and it is not your business to do so. You have, at the most an intuitive knowledge of the human psyche; that may suffice. You wouldn't trust yourself to operate on an appendix, so refrain from operating on a soul.

If you are a juror, don't regard the prosecuting attorney as a superior personality. It has become common practice for most prosecuting attorneys to be interested in "getting" the defendant—that is how they advance their careers. Let the prosecuting attorney talk. And think your own thoughts.

Find out in advance what consequences an affirmative or a negative answer to the questions directed at you will have. Be merciful. Life is hard enough.

Kurt Tucholsky

Where Do We Read Books?

Wo lesen wir unsere Bücher?, 1930

Where indeed?
On the train.

For in this position, moving while seated, a man wants to be entranced, especially if he knows the surroundings as well as does the passenger on the 8.30 a.m. in the morning. That's when he reads the newspaper. But on the way back he reads a book; this he carries in his briefcase (ducks are born with web feet, some nationalities with briefcases). Does man read on the subway? He does. What? Books. Can he read heavy, fat tomes there? Some can. How heavy? As heavy as he can carry. Sometimes things get pretty philosophical on the train. Not so much on the bus—that is designed for lighter reading. Same people also read on the street... like animals.

The books which a man doesn't read while traveling he reads in bed (there follows a lengthy discourse about love and books, books and women, in bed, out of bed—all blue-penciled), in bed, then. Most unhealthy. It certainly is, because the oblique angle at which the eyes look at the book—consult your oculist. Or rather, don't consult him; he will prohibit your nocturnal reading and yet you won't give it up—most unhealthy. In bed, one should indulge in light and entertaining as well as in soothing reading, in addition to the very heavy, scholarly, risqué, medium-heavy, and all other kinds—but that's all.

Then people read their books after Sunday dinner. In about two or two and a half hours one can comfortably snooze away four hundred pages.

Some people read books in a boat or on their own bellies, lying in a green meadow. Especially at this time of year.

Some people, if they're boys, read their books under a school bench. Some people don't read books at all, but review them.

Some people read books on the beach, which makes the books look pregnant. After a week or two they become all bloated—now they're going to give birth to a little pamphlet, you would think—but nothing happens, it's only the sand they have absorbed. There's such a nice rustling sound when you turn a page.

Some people read their books in the... But we've got to say a serious word about that.

Frankly, I'm against that. But I know that many men do it. They smoke and they read while doing it. That isn't good. Listen to an old man—it's no good.

First, because it isn't good, and unhygienic too; it goes against the dignity of the author who has written the book, and after all... Sure, one can think of reading that ought to be done only there, Hitler's *Mein Kampf* and things like that. Because they are useless afterwards, that's how wet they get. One simply shouldn't read books in the bathtub (sigh of relief on the part of the intelligentsia).

Remember: there are only very few situations in any human life in which one cannot, could not, should not read books.

But where are these books produced? That is another story.

Crisis While Reading

Moment beim Lesen, 1932

Sometimes—oh happy moment—you are so engrossed in a book that you are completely immersed in it, dead to the world. Your heart and your lungs are functioning, your body is evenly performing its internal factory work, but you are not aware of it. You are not aware of yourself. You know nothing of the world around you, you hear nothing, see nothing—you are reading. You are under the spell of a book. (This is how an author would like to be read.)

But suddenly the steel bonds loosen a little, the cable from which you have been suspended is lowered a tiny bit. Whether the power of the author has flagged, or he has diminished his intensity because he wanted to save it for another place, or he had a bad morning... suddenly there is a slackening. It is like rising from a dream. To the right and left of the pages the outlines of the room emerge; you go on reading, but with only three-quarters of your concentration; you have an obscure feeling that there is something outside the book: the world. You are still reading. But already the room is pushing its invisible forces toward the book. At this point the book is defenseless; it can no longer stand up to the outside world; imperceptibly you get distracted, you no longer read with both eyes... and you look up.

Hello, room. The room grins inaudibly. You are a bit ashamed. Slightly bewildered, you resume your reading.

But it is no longer as it was before. Outside someone is rattling the kitchen door; the street noises have returned, and upstairs someone is walking back and forth. And now it is quite an ordinary book, just like all the others.

If only one could stick it out like that for two hundred pages! But I suppose no one can.

The Last Page

Die letzte Seite, 1916

My profession (I'm an assistant lighthouse-keeper on a little Baltic island) obliges me to read a lot, for the nights are long. I have no problem getting new books; they are supplied by a friend of mine who is the night editor of the *Bright Beam Bulletin*. He gives me all the review copies he gets, and so I read night after night; all sorts of things, too: novels and travel books and tender emotional tales by noble-minded women authors, and whatever else people write and read.

And when the wind rattles the thick windows, when my burgundy punch is steaming on the table, the tobacco burning in my pipe, and I, old man that I am, think how lucky I am to have held on to this job, it can happen that—because I'm absentminded or just for the fun of it—I start reading a book from the end, just as you sometimes nibble at the raisins before you start eating a cake. And so I've made the discovery that the conclusions of all these books can be clearly divided into various groups. There seem to be standard endings that occur again and again. The author may be a man from Mars, but at the end he does remember his noble humanity and speaks German, you might say.

Tonight I read about four pounds of books again and I still remember quite a bit. So here I go.

THE BESTSELLING LIGHT NOVEL

"I must have felt it for a long time," whispered Helen. "But only you made me conscious of it. Only now am I beginning to live, really live." Edgar folded her in his arms.

So the hours passed without their realizing it. Then they walked hand in hand through the dusky fields over which the tangy smell of new potatoes mingled with the sweet fragrance of the roses.

Edgar Helmenberg took his young sweetheart to the house on the hill. The moon was rising. He took her hand. "Do you see the moon?" he said intensely. "But I will give you the sun!" "The sun!" she whispered, enraptured.

THE UNSUCCESSFUL LIGHT NOVEL

It was all over. Kuno faced the debris of his modest happiness. Why had misfortune struck him? Him, of all people? And the others? Angrily he clenched his fists—and then he dropped his arms again.

There they went. How she had laughed, his—yes, his!—Gertrude. But Doctor Holtzenheimer had money and was a gay blade...

His faithful love, the wooings of all those years—all in vain. He broke down in tears and crushed the rose in his pocket.

THE PROFESSORIAL TRAVEL BOOK

And so we come to the end of my beautiful and instructive journey to Egypt, the Land of the Sun. It has brought me much of novelty and expanded my mental horizon. But it has also proved to me how well-liked Germans are everywhere, if they will only defend their place in the sun. May this little book afford its readers enjoyment and stimulating instruction, so that they, too, may some day go out to the venerable land of the Nile and the kings Ramses and Ramsenit.

It should be added that the medium-sized toadstool mentioned on page 154 has also been observed in Germany. According to Schaedler's account in the *Geographic Weekly*, a scholar in Meissen found one and identified it as such.

NATURALISTIC NOVEL, VINTAGE 1900

"Soul," he whispered. A shot rang out. The frightened apartment-dwellers ran about in confusion; policemen forced a path through the crowd. The man in the corridor was dead. His blood oozed through his left sleeve onto the stone tile floor with its light-blue and greenish pattern and trickled into the dusty crevices.

OLD-TIME NOVEL

"May the Good Lord"—with these words the clergyman closed his speech that deeply moved all those present—"may the Good Lord bless this union which two such mighty families have established through their children."

What else shall I relate? Edward and Kunigunde became a happy couple, but they had many children. The old contention was buried and forgotten. But outside the watchman is already announcing the twelfth hour; so let me extinguish the light, gentle reader, and to all a good night.

A REAL BOYS' STORY: CALIFORNIAN CAMPFIRES

"Blackguard!" The half-breed gritted his teeth. A knife flashed in his hand—but with a tremendous blow the old trapper struck him down.

A short rattling sound—then all was over.

The old trapper escorted the caravan to S., the nearest town; then he went back to his hermitage. "Don't bother to thank me," he said, "I only did what was right."

Frank and Miss Armstrong, the heiress to the treasure of gold, were married and lived happily ever after.

Fred, the waiter, got a suitable job in San Francisco, one he holds to this day.

The crafty Don Pedro was never heard of again; he remains missing.

The old Indian Hefrakorn went to spend the rest of his days with the Kraft family. Frank Kraft has reached a ripe old age, and children and children's children play about his knees. But when he sits around the table with his still beautiful wife, his offspring, and the Old Indian, they often speak about
"Californian Campfires"

*　*　*　*

"All right," I can hear the gentle reader saying, "all that is well and good, but what is a book's ending supposed to be like? Mr. Lighthousekeeper doesn't seem to like any of them."

Well, I must admit that in twenty years of lighthouse reading, I have found only one really good, honest, well-motivated ending in a book. It was in a little volume of poetry by one Herr Hugo Taubensee, entitled *Voices of Spring*. The author, as you could see from his picture on the jacket, was a postman as well as a poet—one of those frequent combinations of business and romanticism. The publisher, of course, was all business. These "Voices of Spring" died away as follows:

Note to the Reader

There are actually more of these collected verses by the author. However, since I lack the funds for additional paper and printing costs, I am forced to break off at this point. But I should be glad to continue the "Voices of Spring" if the sales of this book warrant it. My readers will thus be acting in their own interest if they will buy my book and recommend it to others.

Now that's what I call an ending! But I think I'll turn my attention to beginnings from now on.

Strategic Moment in the Economy

Volkswirtschaftlicher Moment, 1930

I t is—well, how shall I explain it?—it's like this:
"These braces," the little brunette has just said, "these braces are quite soft, they keep getting softer as you wear them, they last indefinitely—oh yes, we sell a lot of them. In fact, they're the only brand we stock—a very good value, a real buy; but if you'd rather have a belt, we have excellent belts, too—this one here, for instance; but as for braces, I can only recommend these…" A pause.

You are undecided.

The light-grey braces are still resplendent beside the nice English belt—both gleam at you pleasantly, as if they were saying: "Here you are, sir." They are really spreading themselves… they are still merchandise.

The merchandise was purchased wisely, on the calculation of the biggest profit. It has been advertised. In the big journals, which manage—with complete independence of the advertising section—to smuggle in a little reading matter among the advertisements, movie starlets bend over antiseptic-looking gentlemen, and the caption reads: "Yes, darling—since you bought a Wonkemeyer belt, I've loved you more." At this moment, everything that is lying before you is still merchandise. But you hesitate.

Hesitate, my friend, and know this: you are at a small apex of your life. One moment, a single moment later, and…

And the belt will no longer be merchandise. It will have become just an ordinary belt. And these will be the consequences of this economic enigma: just a minute ago the belt was still worth five marks and if you hadn't bought it, it would have been bought by some other man whose pants were beginning to fall down. But now, all of a sudden, the belt is nothing at all—it has become your belt, any old belt; the belt has stepped out of the march of merchandise and into your life, and it has suffered in the process.

If, after this little word "yes," this declaration of willingness on your part to accept the offer, which completes the legal transaction of a sale—if you now brought the belt into the same store and wanted to sell your light-brown Wonkemeyer, "the dandy's delight"—why, they'd throw you out. "We don't buy old clothes," the manager would say. Out with you! A belt! What's a belt?

Hesitate, my friend. The saleswoman is still standing in front of you, with a slight stoop of obsequiousness, the whole store seems to be eavesdropping—for there are many such belts at this moment, but not so many buyers, and if a merchant is polite in this world, it always means that the supply exceeds the demand. Hesitate, my friend. Enjoy this moment. Savor its charm to the full, sip it, taste it, delight in it. Remember: if you buy this belt and if you should—pardon the expression—drop dead on your way home, the belt will be among the personal effects in your estate. Not worn yet—but just another belt. Hesitate, keep hesitating; the saleslady is looking at you questioningly. The pause has lasted as long as such a pause can reasonably last. "I'll take this one," you say.

You poor wretch.

From Behind the Venus de Milo

Hinter der Venus von Milo, 1926

B ehind the Venus de Milo in the Louvre in Paris there is a little
bench on which I was sitting the other day. Of the Venus I saw
only her dark, unlighted back. The visitors stood in day—bright
illumination.

There drew near the nations of the earth, at a museum stroll,
already a bit tired from all the walking, and at a distance one could
see the dullness of their faces. But as soon as they approached the
Venus, their expression changed.

Most of them were rather self-conscious and stepped closer with
the kind of face men make when they are wearing a full dress suit
with a somewhat too high collar. They all inwardly snapped to
cultural attention and straightened up. So that's her...! Even the
women often made a half bow—but only if they were alone; some
smiled as though caught in the act. There were also spirits who took
the offensive; they entered the small, high-ceilinged room briskly
and brusquely, as if to say: "Well now, let's see; you really as beautiful as ever'body allus says? Lemme take a look..."

They stepped forward and they stepped back, they looked for a
point de vue and shaded their eyes with their hands in order to
screen out the undue light; they spelled out the little printed plaque
which said that this was the Venus de Milo; I looked into wide open
nostrils and at flashing eyeglasses. Some came up at a quick trot
with something in their eyes that said: "Well now, there you are!"
and: "You hang in our parlor, you know," and: "Really very beautiful!" For some of them there should have been blue and red glasses
with which to make the show more colorful.

Men with heavy treads, rigid carriage, and little hats came up—I
seemed to have seen them before. The only Frenchmen were the

guards, and the loudest thing of all surrounded the quiet statue: the American middle-class lady tourist. Girls from an English boarding school sat on the benches like birds on perches; they were gabbing pretty loudly and passing around sweets and picture postcards. A frightful figure of a foreigner was conversing with a guard who good-naturedly gave him information, with a look that seemed to say: "I've been in this institution for eighteen years and I'm not surprised at anything."

And a pair of lovers on a bench in a corner stayed there for half an hour—here and only here did they feel undisturbed.

And then there came the young generation—athletic types and smooth faces. They looked up at the Venus in quite another way. "The aesthetic value of this body is something eternal"—that's what the art books say. Eternal? Really eternal? Perhaps these young people, whom the saxophone had told a thing or two, thought differently about that. Some sniffed briefly, stood around the pedestal, and went away again. Maybe their kind of Venus looks different.

So I sat there for a long, long time. And this is what I have to say: Personally, I wouldn't want to be the Venus. If glances left spots, she would look like a leopard skin. And how many indifferent eyes look at her! How much convention is about it, how much "must-see," a dutiful stroll through the Louvre. A museum is a thing.

But perhaps one mustn't sit in back of objects at all. For what one gets to see in the course of time soon dulls one, because it is repeated a thousand-fold, because people's imagination is slight and its variety even slighter—and because deep down, judges, physicians, and certain ladies know just how it will happen again—all of it.

Casanova in a Vault

Casanova im Safe, 1928

The publisher Brockhaus of Leipzig owns a Casanova manuscript that has never been published and that he does not
want to publish. I asked him for the reason; he replied courteously
that he didn't care to comment on that.

Legally, everything is quite in order. How and when the manuscript was acquired I don't know; at any rate, Herr Brockhaus owns
all the rights and no one can force him to take out the book and
publish it. As is common knowledge, a work of literature does not
begin to get into the "public domain" until after it has been published. But this undoubtedly interesting volume is lying in a safe
and will presumably continue to lie there for quite a while.

The publisher's motivation in refusing to issue it is not quite ap-
parent; if he considers the work too risqué for his firm, he need only
sell it. The interests of living people can hardly be damaged; no dis-
closures of any sort are to be expected, nor would there be political
repercussions. What is it, then?

It looks to me like a reductio ad absurdum of the principle of private property, which, incidentally, has had a rather deleterious effect
in the field of copyrights. For example, heirs often have positively
catastrophic rights to intellectual property.

Imagine that Friedrich Nietzsche had died without leaving any
relatives. And imagine that friends had taken charge of his works,
and that now there came a woman, one Frau Förster, Elisabeth
Förster, who said: "I'd like to administer Nietzsche's estate. And I
want to write the introduction to his works, too." What would the
friends have said? They would have shrugged their shoulders and
kept silent. A poor, demented person… But now Elisabeth Förster
happens to be Nietzsche's sister, so it's quite all right. She is allowed

to introduce Nietzsche's works, to administer Nietzsche's estate, his letters and his notes—and we all know how she administers them. Still, it didn't do her any good; the real Nietzsche did become known, despite her notorious archives.

But what seems especially dubious to me in the case of Casanova is the actual claim to intellectual ownership on the part of the publisher.

How did he acquire the manuscript? Did he pay for it? Does such a purchase bestow moral rights on him? Did Casanova appoint him or his predecessor the executor of his estate? Is Brockhaus qualified to administer this literary inheritance? Is it one, anyway?

Poor Casanova!

I'm Going Out with a Tall Woman

Ich gehe mit einer langen Frau, 1931

E rica is a bit on the tall side; she knows it and is very unhappy about it. She's exactly four inches too tall.

How I've tried to encourage her! By way of consoling her I told her the story about the tall woman who was sitting in the balcony of the theater; people behind her kept yelling: "Sit down! Sit down, please!" She got up angrily to make those people be quiet, and then somebody cried: "Now the bitch's climbing up the seats!" No comforting her that way.

Then I told her about that other tall lady who was walking along a garden fence and asked the man working in the garden how to get to Eagle's Nest. "Well, just keep riding straight ahead, ma'am," said the gardener. No comforting her that way, either.

But to go walking with Erica is really enjoyable. Not just because she's such a charming person—no; but because I can read the eyes of all passers-by, and that's a great pleasure.

Me, I'm rather short and fat. And Erica is very slim and tall. So when the two of us walk through the streets, people get a kick out of seeing the imposing couple, and I interpret their glances.

The men usually look past us; they have no time. When they do look up, they are happy, but only for a moment—a man is such an ass, he doesn't even know what real joy at somebody else's expense is. And when men are by themselves, they think, and that keeps them quite busy. (But you should just see the results!)

But those women!

It happens in a flash, and I enjoy it immensely. Their eyes say:

"Eureka! A woman who is my inferior! She's too tall. Toby! Mother! Margie! Did you see her? Get a load of her! She's some beanpole, isn't she?" That's a nasty thing to say—Erica isn't a beanpole at all, I know better. But she is four inches too tall and that's a drawback that immediately meets the eyes of those walking women; and I go on reading.

"She's too tall. Hee, hee. I'd like to see her dancing sometime. Or running. Do you suppose the little fat fellow has to get up on a footstool when he wants to kiss her? Lisa, take a look."

Lisa takes a look and agrees. My, it's too good to be true. A woman that tall!

Incidentally, there are nuances, and people's reactions depend on their upbringing. If someone's nursery had a Northern exposure, malicious joy breaks forth unrestrained; in the eyes there glows that little flame of "love-thy-neighbor"; a derisive winking sets in, a winking and a blinking; elbows give neighbors a confidential poke in the side, and two people are as one in the ineffable bliss of taking a swipe at a fellow human being.

People of the better type just throw us a quick look, an almost imperceptible one—but Erica is judged. In this way we contribute a lot to the merriment of our neighbors.

It is incomprehensible how spiteful people can be. It isn't Erica's fault that she is so tall. She is just right for me; I don't find her too tall. And isn't it more than mean to criticize qualities that no one is to blame for?

So there we go and I catch all those glances.

A couple comes toward us. He is of normal size, and she is so dainty, so doll-like, so petite, so unspeakably cute.

I give Erica a poke in the side and shoot Miss Lilliput a quick glance.

"Erica," I say, "did you notice that tiny little woman? Ridiculous. Simply ridiculous. What do you suppose he does when he wants to kiss her—?"

The Bedbugs

Die Wanzen, 1919

Some bedbugs were sitting on the top border of the wallpaper, annoyed by the fact that it was day, a bright, sunny day. There would be daylight for a long time, and so they tried to while away the hours until the good, dark, grey night by discussing their nocturnal plans. From time to time one of the bugs crawled up to the end of the little ledge behind which they were sitting, and looked down at the white bed that stood in the room. They knew that a plump and therefore desirable girl slept in it every night. It was she that they were talking about.

"Me," said the oldest bedbug, "I'm going to crawl around on her head and suck the blood from her temples. Behind the temples there's the brain, you know, and I'm a cultured bedbug. I think I'm getting smarter every day. That's because of the wise thoughts of that she-man down there. I'm a bug on politics."

"Me," said the second bedbug, "I stick more to the fleshy parts. That makes me fat, and I'm the fattest among you. Trade and commerce—that's what we need. I suck the blood from her veins, and she's certainly got plenty of it. I'm a bug on economics."

"Me," said the third bedbug, "when I'm down there, I crawl every which way. I don't need much to eat. I feel fine if I can just crawl around. I look at everything, and everything interests me. You may fatten up your bellies, but I'm up on everything that goes on around this girl. I'm a bug on local affairs."

"Me," said the fourth bug, "I don't eat a thing. I just enjoy looking at the relaxed limbs of the sleeping girl. They're a real treat for my artistic eyes. I'm a bug on esthetics."

"And where are you going?" they asked the last bedbug.

"Me, I'm going to…" said the little fellow.

"Shame on you!" hissed the other bugs.

And so they sat and chewed the fat and flipped their feelers and moved their flat bodies. Then the oldest among them spoke up. "Kids," it said, "it'll be daylight for a long time yet. We've got nothing to do, yet each of us has got a program. What do you say we start a newspaper?"

And so it was done—and when a writer misuses bedbugs like this, it's called an allegory.

Fulfilment

Erfüllung, 1929

The watering of draught horses that have pulled a heavy load—this is what I like to watch. There they stand, with dripping hides; their tails twitch feebly, their heads droop, and one pushes aside the other that is drinking. One can see the water gliding down its throat, being sucked in. Everything about it is greed, sated greed, fresh greed and satiation. Then the second horse drinks, and the first looks around contentedly, with water running from its mouth in long threads... that is beautiful. I should like to caress the teamster who is holding his bucket in front of the horses. Why is that beautiful?

Because it is fulfilled satisfaction, something very rare. It is a legitimate desire, wages worked for, necessity, with a refreshing dash of voluptuousness in it. And it hurts no one. Here no spider is killing the fly, which it has caught with great zeal in order to appease a hunger that is just as natural. And the microbes in our water probably feel no pain; let's not be ridiculous. It is beautiful when horses are being watered.

There is also some joy at human superiority in it—which it is a human being that gives them to drink. If, for example, they drink from a running brook, we don't begrudge it to them, but the picture loses something of the delight with which the first one fills us. As a species we are probably very vain.

And then, too, it is beautiful because horses can't talk. When a thirsty, sweaty-hiker comes up to the bar of a small inn and says, "A large beer! God, what a scorcher," he drinks, and it is hardly an esthetic treat to watch him. If afterwards his eyes shine and he goes "Aaah... ," he seems a trifle silly to those who are not thirsty.

Why it is like that with horses, of all creatures, I don't know. One feels good if one feels good in front of them. A gentle wave of love of animals wells up in you. But this is deceptive.

For afterwards, if the team of horses does not move fast enough, we are angry with the teamster if he does not give them the whip. "*La race maudite, a laquelle nous appartenans...* ," said a certain Fridericus in his native tongue.* If for once we don't happen to be cruel, we are quick to believe that we are good.

---

* An ironic reference to Frederick the Great, who preferred French to his native German.—H.Z.

The Invention of the Zipper

Wie sieht der Erfinder des Reißverschlusses aus?, 1928

The inventor of the zipper I picture as an elderly man who is sometimes cheerful, sometimes morose—cheerful when his wife is out of town, morose at all other times. He has sparse white hair, although he is not that old, a slightly crippled leg, which he drags almost imperceptibly, a conservative pair of glasses, and a low turn-down collar, the kind his grandfather used to wear. He is an American of German descent, and his first name is Sam.

One night Sam cannot fall asleep. It is one of his morose nights, for his wife is lying next to him, looking like an aging glamour girl who has grown fat—not a very happy sight. And Sam isn't happy; he remains turned the other way and is deep in thought. What do you suppose he is thinking about?

Certainly not about inventing a zipper. Sam is neither an engineer nor a technician, but a bookkeeper in a mail-order house for flower seeds. Yet in his spare time he indulges in "do-it-yourself" and, to the great annoyance of the fat glamour girl, fools around with anything he can lay his hands on: the clocks, the radio, the car, the window shutters, even the sacred bathroom fixtures. At present he is interested in his wife's handbag. There is something about it that he doesn't like.

Now the fat glamour girl, half asleep, makes a flabby movement. "Leo," she whispers—that is the name of her first husband. Sam wrinkles his nose; he doesn't like Leo, because Leo is a successful vinegar salesman, wears such high collars, and has a wife who is from down South, with accent to match… . Well, now, the handbag has a clasp, and Mr. Sam don't like this clasp nohow. It just occurred to him: if one could only… and he goes into a brown study.

With a scream the glamour girl starts up from her sleep. "Sam!"

There's no Sam. "There's a burglar in the house!" She hears noises in the kitchen, in the whole apartment. The glamour girl is dying of fright, she comes to again, dies again, and then puts her head with the cute permanent wave under the bed covers, which are designed for just this purpose. Sam is standing in front of her. "What are you screaming about?" he growls darkly. His eyes are shining, he is cheerfully morose.

"Sam! There's a burglar in the house. Did you… ?" "I've got it licked." says Sam. "What have you got licked?" asks the glamour girl. "The clasp problem." "In the middle of the night?" asks the glamour girl. "In the middle of the night." says Sam. He climbs into bed, hearing nothing and seeing nothing, and his old, yellow hands trace such odd patterns on the bed cover that his wife can only shake her head and think of Leo, whom she is glad to be rid of, and of a very different kind of life that she might have had, with someone like Douglas Fairbanks in the morning and Valentino in the afternoon; and because Valentino is dead and Leo is still alive, the glamour girl weeps softly, quite softly. But Sam is smiling.

The next day is Saturday. From Saturday noon to Sunday night Sam sits at his little workbench, banging, hammering, and punching away; then he goes to the little tool shed and beats on the tiny anvil, makes the welding machine hiss, and is awfully busy. On Monday he calls on the manager of a large company who buys his flower seeds from Sam's firm.

"This is where you pull," says Sam. "Look: like this… and here, like that…" The manager says nothing; his hands make movements that are reminiscent of a large bird of prey flapping its wings. "Let me see," he says slowly. And he takes the small leather object studded with bits of metal which Sam hands him. He gives a pull. It is quite still in the small room.

"Why, this is… ," says the manager excitedly, but he composes himself immediately. "This is… hm… this is not useless… not entirely unusable. How much will you take for it?" Figures fly. "Have you got a description of it?" asks the manager. Sam hasn't got one. The manager presses a buzzer. A less fat girl appears. Sam is supposed to dictate, but he can't do it; the manager tries to help. Together they produce a patchwork of a description. The manager is satisfied with it. Sam, who suddenly sees a big fat cheque dancing up and down before his eyes, has a vision, a vision inspired by the less fat glamour girl. He accepts the manager's proposal. Sam, you dumb cluck.

Hardly has Sam left when the manager, armed with a few sheets of paper and the leather object, rushes to the patent office.

At the board meeting faces flush with excitement. "Why, this is… we've never seen… ." There isn't one among these shrewd operators who doesn't smell right off what this is. Hard American heads quickly move back and forth over immaculately knotted neckties. Here is their chance, their big chance. And just when they are about to adjourn, in the firm, secure conviction of having encountered the opportunity of their lives and—God grant that!—utilized it properly, the youngest member of the board asks a question. It is only a brief question, but it produces silence in the room. "What makes it work, anyway?" he asks.

The conversations are chopped off. Yes, come to think of it, just how is it done? Now they all talk at the same time. They all want to find out, but no one knows. Hasty hands leaf through the description which old Sam has dictated and which they have in front of them, neatly mimeographed. But this says only how to work the zipper, not why it works, why, why… . With a vigorous movement the manager lifts up the receiver and gives the operator a number.

"He isn't in?" says the manager. "What do you mean, 'he isn't in'? Tell him to come immediately… . I beg your pardon, madam— your husband is… what? Without telling you? That's very strange. He didn't even come home for lunch, although he usually does?" They look at one another in consternation. And now they all try to explain why a slide fastener, the hope of their lives, works, must work—but they really don't know, nobody knows. Where is the inventor of the zipper?

The inventor of the zipper has cashed his cheque. The inventor of the zipper has left town with a slender, blonde, graceful, divinely made-up glamour girl—bound for Paris. For that's the way it happens in books, the way it happens in the movies. Sam has a pocketful of dollars; the glamour girl has a heart (and all that goes with it) made of celluloid. Now they are floating on the high seas and soon they will be in Paris.

Meanwhile, in America, the first handbags with zippers are on the market and create a sensation. The whole world wants zippers; on tobacco pouches and ladies' handbags, on small suitcases and ministers' briefcases, and it's too bad that they can't be put on all ladies' dresses… . And the competitors tearfully gaze at the little engraved sign on the metal that indicates how well this devilish little trick is protected by law. Never mind! They'll have to wait for the next chance; this one is gone.

And not a soul knows how it is done. No one has an idea of why on earth the zipper works. Nobody knows. The manufacturers can make it, but actually even they aren't quite sure what they are manufacturing. I don't know. You don't know. None of us knows.

And the only human being who does know is sitting, as you read this, in Paris on the corner of Boulevard des Italiens and Rue Helder, selling newspapers. He hasn't got a sou, poor Sam hasn't. The celluloid glamour girl has left him with another Sam whose name is George; his wallet is empty, the dollars have flown away. What is left is a poor, old man, who at night crawls into the little flophouse on Sebastopol Boulevard, where he sleeps in a stuffy room with eight market-district helpers and with just a single, sweet bit of malicious joy in his heart:

He knows what makes the seemingly so simple, world-conquering zipper work. But he isn't talking.

Tenant and Landlord

Mieter und Vermieter, 1929

I don't see that at all. If the pipes are broken, he'll just have to fix them. I've got a contract! A contract... . As a landlord he has an obligation. Why, that would be the limit! It would be... . Let me have the Civil Code... . You know what—I'll give my lawyer a call. As the landlord he's got an obligation; we'll see about that. I'm sorry, but I live here and I simply demand that the pipes in the bathroom be in working order. That's what the man gets his rent for! It's high enough. Come hell or high water, he'll have to fix those pipes... . Here, I'll send him a registered letter... . I'll tell him... I don't see that at all.... I as the tenant... ?"

"I don't see that at all. I as the landlord... ? Those people probably take six baths a day and do their whole wash in the bathtub; no wonder the pipes get broken. I wouldn't dream of repairing them! At my expense? Did you get that? He's going to have them fixed at my expense!

"I'll fix him! At my expense—humph. Let me have the Civil Code... . You know what—I'll simply turn the matter over to the Landlords' Association; let them worry about it... . At my expense! What business of mine is it? He as the tenant... . What I mean is—they're lucky they can live there at all. When you consider how high the taxes are... . And what rent do they pay? A little nothing! I'll tell you something—if we landlords could only do as we please, these people would have been... . Why, I don't see that at all! I as the landlord... ?"

Well and good. The funny thing is not that these monologues and dialogues go something like this; that would be understandable. Both parties are fighting for their money, their interests, their real or imagined rights... that's how it is all over the world.

But that these dialogues go like this and are spoken by the same man—one in the morning, the other in the afternoon—that is one of the purest joys of my life.

For there are people who are tenant and landlord at the same time; in fact, this is quite a common situation. And when they make a decision "as a landlord," they do so with the full aplomb of injured innocence. Someone has violated the most sacred possession a man has—and now the fat is in the fire.

And when these people have before them the very same thing, but the other way round, they carry on so much "as tenants" that a housewife can get scared stiff. And both times they speak in ringing tones of deep conviction.

Trade and traffic afford the best opportunity to study the ideological superstructure, the commercial and the psychological, that we read so much about. Oriental merchants are probably the champions in this; they "prove" to the purchaser that the merchandise is too cheap and to the purveyor that it is too expensive. Logic is put in the service of interests, and if it is harnessed well, it always pulls, pulls the whole works. If you are not much of a logician, you are done for if you get involved.

Note this:

You can prove anything; the fact that you've proved it doesn't prove a thing. There are many syllogisms, many false premises, many false conclusions... . Let them talk, but don't fall into the trap. You will get stuck without fail.

And note further:

You can never appeal to the tenant in the landlord (although he is both in one), nor to the landlord in the tenant. Neither of them has enough imagination for that. They are unable to rethink their own interests; most people have too much of a one-track mind for that. When a man is swimming, he can't play chess; that would be a rarity. And people don't really want to change their thinking. "Where would that get us?" Yes, where indeed? Perhaps to an adjustment of interests? God forbid. Every deal must be negotiated as though the prosperity of the whole world depended on its outcome; if you don't do it that way, you aren't a good businessman. And winning is hard, so hard... . All of us are tenants and landlords. But we slip out of one skin into another as we may require it. In the meantime the old skin hangs there empty and unneeded. The master is not at home… and he bellows vigorously in the other skin; one could almost believe him, one almost could.

Look around and you will see a thousand examples:

A daughter as a mama; an actor as a director; a judge as a defendant; a critic as an author; an employee as an employer. Tenant and landlord, all of them. And no one, not one of them knows that that's what he is.

The Poetry of the Antennas

Lyrik der Antennen, 1931

There is no imagining how they come into being; entire New York neighborhoods must be working on them. And they are pretty much alike, with "I love you" and "blue" and all that stuff. Right now they are probably extra-sentimental. And what is that sentiment like?

They are ready-to-wear lyrics hovering over the big cities, in part they use old forms, but the substance is a throbbing machine heart.

"You make me so sad—you make me so glad." But that isn't true, and the singer doesn't believe it either. He gets good pay if he activates the soft larynx that is needed, and his listeners also know that none of it is true, but it's such nice relaxation after business hours and it's good to dance to. This music sounds so sweet, but if you listen more closely, it is hard as glass and quite brittle. It doesn't give anything; it just wants to be a hit, after working hours.

It goes all over the world and everybody sings it. I am sure one can hear the same tunes in the streets of Canton and Rio de Janeiro. It is music between businesses, not the music of business.... But no, it is the music of business too. If the stock exchange could warble, this is how it would sing.

High above the antennas which broadcast this music quivers the poetry of the world. This music is rootless; it has no fatherland, only a place of manufacture; it wasn't born, it was copyrighted. The man who created it hardly believes in it; the man who deals in it certainly doesn't, and neither does the listener, really... It is an article of use—like chewing gum.

Yet sometimes I wonder: what are the people like who listen to this stuff in the evening? What are we like, then?

They are people who live in the city and have no garden. But sometimes they look with emotion at a little artificial garden of fabric flowers and papier-maché trees inside a glass globe, and the hands of these people move over that smooth ball with a tenderness they normally don't expend… that is their poetry. Actually, they don't give it any further thought, and certainly not a thought as complicated as this.

"Please turn on the phonograph, Barbara!" And Barbara turns it on.

A hair-oil voice rings out; the fellow who is singing fairly whimpers from his throat; he has a bed timbre, so to speak, and love oozes out of him like velvet, for he has received a good-sized cheque. It is a very impersonal tenderness that flows from this voice, directed at no one, and that is why everyone is very touched—slightly touched in the head, that is. And because the music goes "chuck-chuck, chuck-chuck-chuck," people do a little dance to it—in a studio or some other place. What's the man singing?

Industrious young ladies, who haven't anything else to do, sit in front of the phonograph with pencil and paper, taking down the key words, those combinations of "I love you" and "happiness," an ever-changing kaleidoscope. That's fame for you; look how they jot things down and have the record played for them sixty-four times so as not to miss a single precious word! And when they've managed to make it all out and take everything down, they go and lose the slip of paper; but by now they know the text by heart and sing along—until there is a new lyric in which the singer assures everyone that he is happy because he is so sad, and all because of you-ou-ou… Someone sings and says "golden June moon," but there's no gold and no June and no moon… that's how nice these songs are.

But one must never listen to this functional music, which has always been around, with ordinary ears. It takes a very special kind of ear to absorb it completely. Functional music is understood only by those who experience it directly. That's why it is impossible to refurbish old operettas completely; even parts of Offenbach's works are dusty, passé, empty-sounding despite all their musical charm. Why? Because we don't go backstage in a top hat any more and no longer give rings to little chorus girls. Because the forms of love have changed—not the sexes, but the style. These old waltzes suddenly sound so simple, but they never were. The composer of this music-for-use just hadn't been able to put everything into his hit; he poked his contemporaries with his elbow and winked at them: "You know, don't you… you know…" And his contemporaries knew. We no longer do.

But we do know exactly what the score is on those American song hits. These songs pretend to be dumb; it is the utmost shrewdness with which, say, a very elegant lady puts on "a very simple dress"; there's nothing to it, you know, it's extremely simple. Costs a lot of money, that dress. These songs seem to be childlike, simple, youthful, but they're none of these things. They are as old as the hills, sad, pitifully empty, because everything has been pumped into them…. Love made of tin. And yet there is something to them.

It is the spirit of the times, the spirit of 1931, the mood of overworked people when they want to relax in the evening by not relaxing. Feelings crumble, something soars, someone sings about her beautiful brown eyes, but they are the eyes of a rocking horse, it's all a farcical, puppet kind of love, and yet everything is genuine, because it is so gloriously false.

But high above the antennas which disseminate this music quivers the poetry of the world.

Four Ways of Looking at a Squirrel

Viermal Eichhörnchen, 1932

THE FACTS

On the path through the park sits a squirrel. As it catches sight of me, it sits up and begs and then runs up to me. It looks at me, then climbs up on me. It is probably accustomed to being given nuts or sugar, but I don't have any. It runs down again, sits at my feet for a moment, and then runs away.

THE SQUIRREL: A NATIONALISTIC VIEW

I take a German walk through our German forest. My German eyes observe the wonderful German landscape and are carried away by its magic. From this clearing one could quite easily launch a general attack; that meadow would make a fine field of fire for a covered machine gun. And there—what is that? The enemy. Mechanically I take cover. It is a squirrel, a German squirrel. Blond like Goebbels, it twitches its tail playfully. But what's this? It does not run away. A German does not run away. Instead, it runs up to me, the dear little creature, sniffs at me, and now, now, it really and truly climbs up on me, just like a squirrel. It looks at me with its shiny eyes, as if it wanted to say: "Do you not agree that the disgrrraceful Treaty of Versailles is a blot on the German escutcheon of German honor?"

And fearsomely, hugely, before my inner eye this animal grows into a symbol of German greatness: it, too, will some day avenge us and our children and children's children on the French. And I can see the squirrel, harnessed to a tank, move forward in the service of the National Cause for which all of us, every last man and maiden, bear our children.

For what do the Germans supply the world with? Human jam.

THE SQUIRREL: A MOTION PICTURE

Anny, a playgirl, is in love with Adolf, a "heavy." Anny has a good middleclass background that unfortunately has deteriorated because of the bad times. One of her two brothers is a motion picture executive, and the other brother also belongs to the underworld. Anny loves Adolf, with whom she takes cocaine, which Bertold, a crooked dope peddler, supplies her with (but we watch him adulterating it with tooth powder, which makes it harmless; how the tooth powder is adulterated we don't get to see). Bertold is also in love with Anny, unbeknownst to Adolf, who loves a certain Milly, who loves a fellow named Max, who is in love with a girl called Caroline. All Milly knows is that Max is not in love with Bertold. Now we see, in between sumptuous parades along the waterfront, how everything builds up to a catastrophe.

In the end Anny sits disconsolately on the trunk of a willow and sobs away, asking herself what one thing has to do with another and why the picture is called "The Squirrel."

We need not add that all screening committees have designated this film as "culturally valuable."

THE SQUIRREL AS VIEWED
BY A CHILD PSYCHIATRIST

Case No. 168. A seven-year-old boy comes to my office because his parents have strictly forbidden him to do so. Posturologically he is the prototype of a boy made biocentric by the effect of an emotional syndrome.

After protracted questioning I establish the following.

About four weeks ago the boy walked through the nearby town forest alone and there encountered a squirrel. The animal first climbed up on him (!), then threatened him, and finally was frightened by the child's screams and ran away.

From this statement it is quite clear that here is a case of a child spoiled by his parents and unable to cope with life. He simply wants to be the focus at all times; even the animals of the forest (memories of picture books!) are supposed to pay attention to the boy (cf. Dr. S. Popelreuther's study *Susie, a Schizophrenic Squirrel*).

Purely from the standpoint of vocational psychology, the intellectual focus of this boy may be sought in the problem of his social relatedness to his non-libidinous environment, but we must beware of throwing our therapeutic pedagogy into the libido-energetic pot of psychoanalysis.

His psychic capacity urges the boy on to play (cf. Prof. Dr. Fritz Giese, *Guide to the Erection of Clinical-Psychological Bowling Alleys*). This child has as yet no knowledge of non-knowledge. He unfortunately misinterpreted my invitation to tension-reduction and responded by peeing in his pants. The only regrettable feature is the fact that the squirrel involved did not appear at my office. With the aid of clinical psychology the degenerate animal could have been turned into the ideal of mankind: a good nursemaid.

THE SOPHISTICATED SQUIRREL

We are walking through the park full of summer snow; next to me is Cardinal Rosenberg, the kindly financial adviser to the Pope, as well as the most beautiful woman of South America, Countess Oça-Jolly. In lively alternation we chat about the finances of Uru- and Paraguay as well as the enchanting roadsters we saw at the auto exhibition in Colombia; we wouldn't have it any other way. A bobsled bearing the Swiss Baron Von Moegli-Taegli whizzes past us and we wave greetings.

Then the beautiful woman, who is wearing a peacock-grey velvet sports jacket with a small trimming of silver lame, emits a soft scream: His Eminence, too, seems moved.

"Sefiora Conchita!" I cry. "What's doing?" cries the Cardinal.

Suddenly everything turns black with diagonal spots before my eyes. I can still see a huge animal about to take a diving leap at me. "Bears!" I think quick as a flash—but it could also be a bison. With bold determination I hurl myself backward four to eighteen paces, and then peals of genuine silver laughter hit my ears. The Countess is calling out the name of the animal—it is a squirrel!

It is, of course, an especially elegant specimen of its kind. It has two nimble eyes, twitches about timidly like a newspaper publisher, and is flashily dressed. The Cardinal makes one of those signs of benediction to which he is accustomed from the stock exchange. "Don't scare it away, Your Eminence," I beg him. We stand still.

The squirrel climbs up on Countess Oça-Jolly, sniffs the fragrance of her well-groomed eyebrows, and then hurries on to the nearest tree, for lunch. Through the branches beckons the villa of the great industrialist Bergius, who was narrowly snatched from starvation by the bestowal of the Nobel Prize. In the background one can see Gerhart Hauptmann in golf pants and pregnant with a new play.

For even though the world may go to pot, one thing will exist forever: the international set.

Conversation in Limbo

From: Nachher, 1925–1928

We were floating on the waves—short and long waves wafted about us, supplied by the broadcasting stations of the planets for our men's bath in the beyond. Muted screaming was coming from the family cabins.

"What was your worst impression here with us?" he asked. I said: "The first day in the receiving room—that was horrible. I don't even want to think back to it, it was that horrible."

"Why?' he asked.

I answered: "Seventy-two years on earth, that means: sixty-nine years of lying, concealed emotions, hypocrisy; of grinning instead of biting; of scolding where you felt love… . Sometimes you get a presentiment that perhaps you'd better leave it off. "Conscience," the religious leaders call it. But it's only the feeble ebbing away of the feeling that those who have died before us see right through us from on high. Just imagine: all the lies revealed! If I had known that! I came into the receiving room and thought the earth would have to swallow me up for shame. But there was no earth. Terrible—never in my whole life was I so ashamed, so terribly ashamed. And the worst of it all was that they merely looked at me. They all just looked at me. No one returned to those embarrassing things—but I knew just the same that they knew everything. I was small as a mouse, and as miserable. I would never lie again."

"The old man who arranges these things," said he, "should have advanced that ceremonial of the receiving room, put it before our life. Then, perhaps…"

"Yes," I said.

"But then it wouldn't have been so beautiful," he said.

"No," I said.

A big wave came now, one of the long, powerful ones, and threw our legs together, so that we had to laugh.

We were sitting on a cloud, swinging our legs.

"What I liked best all my life," I said, "were the establishments that were a bit rotten. That's where I liked to work. With the boss a little "gaga," as the French say, senile, not quite on the ball anymore—an alcoholic, perhaps. His assistant a good-natured fellow who didn't have too much to say. No one did, in fact—the idea of a superior had fallen into disuse. People didn't worry much about rules, either—they were on the books, but didn't bother anybody. Those places always had something morbid about them, they were coming to an end—a quiet decay. You know—people worked, they didn't loaf, there was business; but, on the whole, it was only going through the motions of working. Did you ever see a chorus girl with a bit part in a farce swab off the furniture? That's what it was like. It was awful when things were supposed to be freshened up, when a new man came who said on the very first day: "This mess is going to be cleaned up!" How long it always took the new man to get broken in! Because decay is contagious—that's undeniable. In seventy-two years I never found any exception to that. That's right. There are lots of places of that kind. I found them in the Army and in industry; in the country there were estates like that—right out of an operetta. Nice working there. Very nice. And always that slight tickle of fear of the end that had to come sometime—it couldn't go on like that forever."

"No," he answered, "of course it couldn't. By the way, are you coming to the Good Lord's this afternoon?"

"Who's going to be there?" I asked.

He answered: "Gandhi, one of the Unknown Soldiers, and some new fellow."

"I don't like new fellows," I said. "They have such an air of solemnity about them." Then we swung our legs again.

"Did you ever learn to swim—that time when you were alive?" I asked him. We were floating through space, in colorless light; actually there was no sense in moving, because there was no determining where we were going. No planets were to be seen—they were rolling along in the distance.

"No," he said. "I can't swim. I had a hernia—my body was rup-tured."

"I didn't learn it either," I said. "I always wanted to and started three or four times, but nothing ever came of it. Same thing with French. Did you accomplish everything you planned to? Neither did I. And then—on quiet evenings, when you were able to catch your breath and the whole claptrap of the daily grind had faded away, there came those thoughtful hours and those good intentions. Did you ever have that feeling?"

"I sure did," he said. "And often!"

"So did I," I said. "You planned such a lot of things on such evenings. That's when it became clear that, when you came right down to it, you were occupied with a lot of nonsense that didn't do anybody any good, least of all yourself. Those childish invita-tions! Those utterly useless meetings at which they chewed over for the hundredth time what you already knew; those eternal sermons to those who were already convinced... . That senseless rushing around town on errands that served no other purpose than to send you on fresh errands the next day... . How much drudgery was at-tached to every single thing, how much labor, how much torture... . The purpose of things was completely forgotten; they had become independent and dominated us. And if, by way of exception, it be-came quite still around you, so still that you could hear the silence ringing in your ears, you swore that you'd start a new life."

"You even believed it," he said sadly.

"And how!" I went on eagerly. "You went to bed, quite full of this beautiful resolution to clear away all this nonsense and live your own life—your very own. And to study. To learn everything you missed, to catch up, to overcome that old laziness and lack of will-power. French, swimming, and the rest. But in the morning your lawyer called, then Aunt Jenny and the secretary of your club, and it had you again. Then it was all over."

"Did you lead the life you wanted to lead?" he asked and didn't wait for an answer. "Of course you didn't. You led the life they de-manded of you—tacitly, by agreement. You would have offended everybody if you hadn't done it, you'd have lost your friends, been isolated, rated as a ridiculous hermit. 'He is crawling into his shell,' they would have said. A dirty word! Well, that's past. And if you were born now, how would you act?"

He stopped his swimming motions and looked at me intently.

"In exactly the same manner," I said, "the very same."

"What did you laugh at?" I asked him. It had been a rather peculiar laugh, a sort of sob, midway between laughter and crying.

"I laughed," he said, "because I had to think of down below. Of something very definite; it's quite stupid. You know, today is the anniversary of my death—no, don't congratulate me, it's hardly worth mentioning. Wait for my fiftieth, my good man, my fiftieth. Eight years ago today. Do you know why the living are not afraid of dead people who have just died?"

"I can imagine it," I said. "Because—because for some time we are tied down, not up here yet—well, you know. It is as if they suspected that."

"Quite right," he said. "That's the way it is. We are not immediately available—they are safe from us, right afterwards. Well, all right—and you know, don't you, what happens to our belongings afterwards."

"Of course I do," I replied. "They take an inventory; then the heirs come running, the children, the creditors…"

"The inventory is what I was just thinking of," he said. "That is, not precisely the inventory, but the way they poke about in our things. It's comical and touching at the same time. It's this way. They empty out the drawers, scratch around at the cupboard locks, unpack everything and then put it back again… Every trouser button suddenly has significance, every penknife is loaded with sentimentality, old stamps wear expressions of grief and share in the mourning. They find old envelopes with prescriptions and cigar ashes in them; quinine tablets and neatly-kept theatre programs with which we were going to do something someday, but of course we forgot, and now all this rubbish is lying in our drawers; one fourth of all human belongings usually consists of such junk. And they touch all that with trembling fingers and their tears drop on it; and as they open and close account books and sniff glass stoppers, they keep saying: "Oh, he kept that!" and "He always used to like agate stones so much!" And all of a sudden our being is distributed among a thousand items that are staring at them—we are looking at them with a thousand eyes. Everything comes to their minds again, comes alive… they never loved us that way."

"No," I said, "they never did."

"What's the reason for that?" he asked cautiously.

"I suppose one has to be gone in order to be loved," I said.

"Not yet there or gone; one must wish in order to love. In our lifetime no one worries about our estate."

"But at that time it isn't an estate yet," he said.

"Did you ever look into your Book of Life?" he asked.

"It was the biggest surprise I've ever had," I said. "It's certainly the limit."

"I'll say! To write down how often you committed each and every act!"

"The other day I spent a whole afternoon in the library, leafing through my volume. It's very accurately kept, I must admit. Some things I wouldn't have considered possible. In its totality it does look different from what it did when you were doing it. Hunted for your keys: 393 times. Smoked a cigarette: 11,876 times. Smoked a cigar: 1078 times. Cursed: 454 times (cursing is permitted in our country, that's why I wasn't so good at it; after all, I'm not an Englishman). Given alms to a beggar: 205 times. Not often. Eaten nougat (would any man ever think of writing that down?): 3 times. I have no idea what nougat is. But the bookkeeper's handwriting is so neat that it must be correct. Incidentally, the last thousand pages were written on a bookkeeping machine. Things are being modernized… The strangest part of it is to think that you did this or the other thing for the last time in your life. Certainly, some occasion must have been the last time. On February 14th of some year you got into a car for the last time. And, of course, you have no idea. After all, a finale you get only in an opera. You get into an automobile quite comfortably, drive, get out—and don't know that this was to be the last time. For then, perhaps, you fell ill, were bedridden for a long time—never again to ride in a car. You've eaten sauerkraut for the last time in your life; for the last time made a phone call; for the last time made love; for the last time read Goethe. Maybe this was years before your death. And you don't know it."

"But it's a good thing one doesn't know it," he said. "Isn't it?"

"Perhaps," I answered. "Anyway, in every action one performs one ought to think: Do it well. Put yourself into it completely. Perhaps it is your last time."

Afterword
What May Satire Do? Anything

By Steven Zohn

"Where are the great satirists of today?," my father Harry Zohn often asked rhetorically as I was growing up during the 1970s and 1980s. It was a good question, for satire seemed to have lost its edge and even its cultural visibility during much of the six decades he spent in the United States. Not that there wasn't plenty of raw material for satirists during this era: the Vietnam war, the Watergate scandal, and the cynical policies of the Reagan administration come immediately to mind as low points crying out for high-satirical treatment by a modern-day Kurt Tucholsky. But satirists such as Tucholsky, whom my father saw as combining a "mordant depiction of human nature with an altogether humanistic and humanitarian intent," were in his view no longer possible, now that "the bedrock of sanity which must serve as the launching pad for their satirical barbs has turned into quicksand." Tucholsky's question and answer "What may satire do? Anything" ("Was darf die Satire? Alles.") is not being taken seriously.

Translating Tucholsky was therapeutic for my father, who admitted that "not a day goes by when I don't think ... which *bon mot* would Tucholsky have said." Satire was for him a *conditio humana*, a "bridge over the abyss," and he occasionally indulged his own satiric streak, closely tethered to his well-known proclivity for puns. (I still have a copy of his satirical open letter to the fictitious "Leonardo Pescatore" about the New England Aquarium's Proud Parent Program, urging him to "adopt" piscene personages such as the aquatic-operatic couple Porgy and Bass. And then there was his homage to the Marx Brothers, the Dontist family of Endo, Ortho, Perio, and Prostho, as comedic as they were costly.) If my father would have been horrified by the Ages of Bush and Trump, he would doubtless have taken some solace in satire's consequent revival "in these great times" (to quote the title of a speech given by Karl Kraus, Tucholsky's Viennese counterpart, following the outbreak of World War I).

But the story I wish to tell here really goes back to the time of Tucholsky, when Harry Zohn was a middle-class Jewish boy growing up in the Vienna of the 1920s and '30s, forming a life-long attachment to what he would later call a "city of miracles and signs" or "Serendipity City." Vienna was then at a historical and political crossroads, even as the afterglow of its fin-de-siècle golden age still shone as a cultural beacon. If the city's literature held a particular attraction to my father in these early years, its music took hold of him with "exceptionally evocative auditory tentacles": Strauss-family waltzes, Bruckner's and Mahler's symphonies, and Wiener-lieder (songs celebrating Vienna)—all of which would form a kind of soundtrack in my own childhood home some forty years later. His cultural attachment to Vienna became physical detachment after he and his family joined the ranks of "thirty-eighters" who fled Austria in the wake of the Anschluss (traveling to England in 1939 before settling permanently in Boston the following year), and then finally morphed into a psychological "love with detachment," as he earned degrees at Suffolk, Clark, and Harvard Universities on the way to a distinguished forty-five-year career as a professor of German language and literature at Brandeis University.

Love with detachment or love from a distance is a concept my father borrowed from the novelist and essayist Max Brod, who coined the word "*Distanzliebe*" to describe his relationship to Germany and to German culture. It encapsulated his attitude toward the people and culture of present-day Austria, just as a quotation from the psychologist Alfred Farau described his outlook as an émigré: "Emigration is a rupture in life, a lifelong rupture. For home is a horoscope. One can change one's residence, of course, but not one's childhood home" ("*Emigration ist ein Bruch im Leben, ein lebenslanger. Denn Heimat ist ein Horoskop. Man kann zwar seine Wohnung wechseln, aber nicht sein Elternhaus*"). My father's complex love for the home of his youth is also captured in the title to one of his books: "I am a son of the German language only"

("*Ich bin ein Sohn der deutschen Sprache nur*"), taken from a poem by fellow thirty-eighter Ernst Waldinger.

From the age of sixteen, Harry Zohn fully embraced the United States as his new home, taking to heart Goethe's words from *Wilhelm Meisters Lehrjahre*, "My fatherland is where I can be of service / do some good" ("*Wo ich nütze, ist mein Vaterland*"). "I have learned," he wrote in a 1998 essay published posthumously in 2009, "to appreciate this bilingualism and biculturalism, a cultural mediation which constitutes, in some respect, a dual citizenship." Although his native language was not standard German, but rather "that same mixture of Galician Yiddish and Viennese dialect which so thoroughly horrified Karl Kraus," he became a professor of German to teach and, in his own words, to:

> "maintain, protect and mediate to new generations the literary, cultural and ethical values contained in that language. ... Simply put, I did not want to be robbed of my native language. ... In America I could learn something of what Jews have contributed to the culture of Vienna ... gain an aftertaste of it and reconstruct it. ... I still see myself today as a literary, cultural and human mediator."

My father's activities as a literary and cultural mediator began with his doctoral dissertation at Harvard ("Stefan Zweig as a Mediator in Modern European Literature") and continued with his subsequent work as a writer, editor, and translator impelled to interpret and preserve Austrian- and German Jewish literature. The Jewish side of this equation was crucial, as he himself participated in the peculiarly Jewish (and perhaps unholy) fascination with the German language and the values embodied in it, which makes the much-discussed German Jewish symbiosis the most tragically unrequited love affair in world history. Long ago I raised the question whether cultural mediatorship may be regarded as an eminently Jewish trait and answered it with a qualified "Yes." Nor should the human aspect be underestimated, since his ties to literature and culture were forged not so much by "authors, works, themes, ideas, or currents," but by "very special people whom it was my good fortune to befriend."

199

Among these special people was Mary Gerold-Tucholsky (1898–1987), the writer's second wife; I fondly recall meeting her at her home in the Bavarian town of Rottach-Egern on the Tegernsee during a family vacation to Europe in 1978. Some years later, the first edition of *Germany? Germany!* was dedicated to the memory of this "noble and gracious lady who was for decades the ideal guardian of both the letter and the spirit of Kurt Tucholsky's work."

Translating is a difficult and poorly paid profession, as my father freely admitted, but for him it was primarily a labor of love rather than one of necessity. More than once I heard him express gratitude that Brandeis considered his translations as equivalent to research, and to be sure, he approached translating with the same dedication, creativity, and "*Sitzfleisch*" (staying power) that he applied to his own writings, whether scholarly or journalistic. And yet, when asked if he kept first drafts of his finished translations, he replied that he had never taken himself so seriously. Besides, he added, if he had hung on to his drafts, his work space would look even worse than it did! This reminds me of my childhood forays down to the basement to visit my father, who was usually seated at the typewriter in his claustrophobic, book-lined study (a "book-crypt," in his formulation): occasions of wonder. "I just came down to do some tipping," I once remarked as a toddler, much to my father's delight (as he never tired of recounting to me in later years).

Despite his considerable professional success over more than half a century, Harry Zohn retained a certain amount of humility about translating prose into a language other than his mother tongue: "If one comes to a country at fifteen, and then fifty years later still has an accent when speaking English, and doesn't have the in-your-sleep certainty of a native speaker…," his answer to an interviewer trailed off. "But I nevertheless believe I have the right to translate into English. … I think I am bilingual insofar as such a thing is possible." Occasionally he asked my mother Judith and, eventually, myself and my sister Marjorie (an actress and director who picked up my father's love of the theatre) whether a particular English phrase he was considering as a translation sounded idiomatic. From this I gained an appreciation for the care he took in providing not just an accurate translation of the original text, but one that also conveys that text's linguistic flavor and cultural resonances to a new audience. Doing so effectively, in my father's view, might entail taking liberties with the author's words (as, for instance, with his translation of "A Fable" in this volume). "In the case of Tucholsky," he observed, "I have sometimes made word-plays that he didn't make."

I like to think that Tucholsky's way with language helped inspire my father's own tongue-in-cheek literary project during his first years of retirement. Asked to contribute some "shuffle rhymes" ("*Schüttelreime*"; better known in English as spoonerisms) to an edited volume, he ended up writing and self-publishing a collection of 350 couplets and short poems (*In Kürze gewitzelt, / Mit Würze gekitzelt* [Boston: Edition Harryzohna, 1997]). Most are in German, since that language is better suited than English to such shufflings, but a fair number are bilingual and several are in English. As this poetic form really is untranslatable, I offer here three of the English rhymes: "Couch Potato: If you feed your hubby chips / He will soon have chubby hips"; "New York Statesman: I saw graffiti at the Finger Lakes: / 'At this antique store you needn't linger. Fakes!'"; and "Gunboat Diplomacy: The negotiations fell short. / The next command was this: 'Shell fort!'"

Satire, to return to my original topic, presents special challenges to the translator, as my father noted in a 1993 essay on translating Tucholsky and Kraus: "The fact remains that it is impossible to convey the full force of satirists whose work is to such large extent tied to their own language; yet enough can be Englished to bring out the universal relevance of their satire and perhaps even some of their craftsmanship." If satire deploys "humor as a weapon," as the American writer Max Eastman put it, then the translator of satire, according to my father, "must actually fashion a carefully crafted weapon in another language, one made of other material, and must see to it that it is not blunted in transit and has comparable sharpness." He viewed this directive as among the translator's foremost commandments: "Keep faith with the satirist; join him (if need be, across continents and ages) as an equal partner in the forging of an effective weapon made of language; be, so to speak, on the same wavelength; be scrupulously attentive to the satirist's methods and purposes."

My father would surely have been pleased to see this new edition of *Germany? Germany!*, which he considered the best of his Tucholsky readers. The book's first edition, *Germany? Germany!: The Kurt Tucholsky Reader,* edited by Harry Zohn (Manchester: Carcanet, 1990), with translations by Harry Zohn (prose), Karl R. Ross (poetry), and Louis Golden (chansons), was based in large measure on two earlier volumes: *The World is a Comedy: A Tucholsky Anthology,* translated and edited by Harry Zohn (Cambridge, MA: Sci-Art, 1957); and *What If – ? Satirical Writings of Kurt Tucholsky,* translated and edited by Harry Zohn and Karl F. Ross (New York: Funk & Wagnalls, 1967). *The World is a Comedy,* which included a few translations published as early as 1955–56, opened with a brief preface in which my father proudly called attention to the project's novelty: "I consider it a real privilege to have this opportunity of introducing Kurt Tucholsky to the English-speaking world. Except for my translations, virtually nothing by him has appeared in English." Sixty years hence, the translations of the present volume not only trace the chronological arc of Tucholsky's writings available in English, but also of my father's efforts to champion writers and writings representing the German- and Austrian Jewish experience. More importantly, and as he observed shortly after the first edition's appearance, "such delicacies" as Tucholsky's satirical writings deserve a wider English-speaking audience than they have so far enjoyed. This is arguably more true today than it was in the 1990s, for as ominous waves of nationalistic populism sweep across America and Europe, threatening to weaken democratic institutions in their wake, the ever-timely words of Tucholsky offer both humorous comfort and a stern warning.

Steven Zohn has published widely on eighteenth-century music and is a noted performer on historical flutes. He lives in Philadelphia with his son, Elliott Harry Zohn, and is Laura H. Carnell Professor of Music History at Temple University, Pennsylvania.

presents

2010–2017 Program

Subscribe to our newsletter at www.berlinica.
com and get one of the e-books below for free.

New in 2017

Cornelia Dömer

MARTIN LUTHER'S TRAVEL GUIDE

500 YEARS OF THE 95 THESES.

ON THE TRAIL OF THE

REFORMATION IN GERMANY

Softcover, 176 pp., full color
120 pictures and 14 maps, $13.95

ISBN: 978-1-935902-44-7

Kurt Tucholsky

BERLIN! BERLIN!
DISPATCHES FROM THE WEIMAR REPUBLIC

Preface by Anne Nelson
Introduction by Ian King

Softcover, 198 pp., 41 pictures, $13.95
ISBN: 978-1-935902-23-2

"... the most brilliant, prolific, and witty cultural journalist of his time"

Kurt Tucholsky

RHEINSBERG
A STORYBOOK FOR LOVERS

WITH: AMONG CITY WIZARDS
Afterword by Peter Boethig

Hardcover, 96 pp., 35 pictures, $14.95
ISBN: 978-1-935902-25-6

"This book was the blueprint for love for an entire generation"

Kurt Tucholsky

PRAYER AFTER THE SLAUGHTER
POEMS FROM WORLD WAR I

Bilingual Edition, translated by Peter Appelbaum and James Scott

Softcover, 116 pp., 6 pictures,
$12.95, ISBN: 978-1-935902-28-7

"He heaped scorn on the reactionary institutions of the old regime"

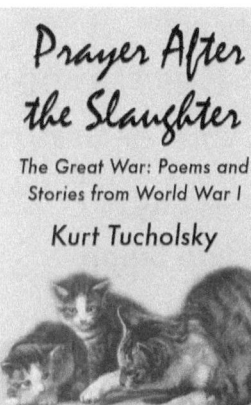

Andreas Austilat
MARK TWAIN IN BERLIN
NEWLY DISCOVERED STORIES & AN ACCOUNT OF TWAIN'S BERLIN ADVENTURES
Preface by Lewis Lapham

Softcover, 176 pp., 67 pictures, $13.95, ISBN: 978-1-935902-95-9

"This fascinating book is a must-read for any Twain enthusiast"

Sebastian Ringel
LEIPZIG!
ONE THOUSAND YEARS OF GERMAN HISTORY
BACH, LUTHER, FAUST: THE CITY OF BOOKS AND MUSIC

Softcover, 224 pp., color, $25.95
ISBN: 978-1-935902-58-1

"Humorous and touching stories from thousand years of Leipzig"

Erik Kirschbaum
BURNING BEETHOVEN
THE ERADICATION OF GERMAN CULTURE IN THE UNITED STATES IN WORLD WAR I
Preface by Herb Stupp

Softcover, 176 pp., 20 pictures, $14.95, ISBN: 978-1-935902-85-0

"Powerful retelling of a forgotten piece of American history"

Michael Brettin/Peter Kroh

BERLIN 1945
WORLD WAR II:
PHOTOS OF THE AFTERMATH

From the Soviet Army Archives

Preface by Steven Kinzer

Softcover, 218 pp., 177 bw photos
$25.95, ISBN: 978-1-935902-02-7

"Even if you think you've seen it all, Berlin 1945 will surprise you"

Thomas Flemming

BERLIN IN THE COLD WAR–THE BATTLE FOR THE DIVIDED CITY

Softcover, 90 pp., $11.95
51 pictures, 3 maps
ISBN: 978-1-935902-80-5

"The story of a divided city in a nutshell, without missing a beat"

Michael Cramer

THE BERLIN WALL TODAY
REMNANTS, RUINS REMEMBRANCES

Softcover, 100 pp., $15.95
Full color, 150 pictures,
ISBN: 978-1-935902-10-2

"A well-illustrated book"

Erik Kirschbaum

ROCKING THE WALL

BRUCE SPRINGSTEEN: THE BERLIN CONCERT THAT CHANGED THE WORLD

Softcover, full color, 168 pp., 45 pict.,
$16.95, ISBN: 978-1-935902-82-9

"A clear statement of the power of music"

**Andreas Nachama
Julius Schoeps
Hermann Simon**

JEWS IN BERLIN

Preface by Carol Kahn-Strauss

Softcover, 314 pp., $25.95
376 pictures,
ISBN: 978-1-935902-60-7

". . . a captivating read that promises a wealth of enjoyment . . ."

Holly-Jane Rahlens

WALLFLOWER

A BERLIN NOVEL

Softcover, 146 pp., $12.95
ISBN: 978-1-935902-70-6

". . . an absorbing story of two people who are trying to figure out who they are and a fascinating look at the dawning of a new era in Germany . . ."

Monika Maertens

BERLIN FOR FREE

A GUIDEBOOK TO MOVIES, MUSEUMS, MUSIC, AND MORE FOR THE FRUGAL TRAVELER

Softcover, 104 pp., $11.95
ISBN: 978-1-935902-40-9

"This book is an investment that pays for itself—whoever wants, or has to save, needs it"

Lothar Heinke

WINGS OF DESIRE ANGELS OF BERLIN

Softcover, 102 pp., $19.95
Full color, 123 pictures
ISBN: 978-1-935902-18-8

"A book full of anecdotes about the angels throughout the city– and a search for angelic traces"

Rose Marie Donhauser

THE BERLIN COOKBOOK

TRADITIONAL RECIPES AND NOURISHING STORIES

Hardcover, 104 pp., $21.95
61 recipes, 98 color pictures
ISBN: 978-1-935902-51-5

"Beautiful pictures, entertaining texts, and easy to process, fresh ingredients"

Adrienne Haan

BERLIN – MON AMOUR

A TRIBUTE TO 1920s GERMANY IN MUSIC

Music CD, 50 minutes
In English or German
$ 15.95, only on Amazon

"Grace, elegance, power"

Rosemarie Reed

THE PATH TO NUCLEAR FISSION

NARRATED BY LINDA HUNT

Movie DVD, run time 81 min
German / English, subtitled
$19.95, only on Amazon

"... honors the lives of women who were more than significant ..."

Stefan Roloff

THE RED ORCHESTRA

A DOCUMENTARY ABOUT THE GERMAN ANTI-NAZI RESISTANCE

Movie DVD, run time 57 min.
German and English, subtitled
$24.95, only on Amazon

". . . danger invaded normalcy . . . landscape threatens to tumble . . ."